JOSEF P. KLEIHUES

JOSEF P. KLEIHUES

THE MUSEUM PROJECTS

EDITED BY KIM SHKAPICH

RIZZOLI
NEW YORK

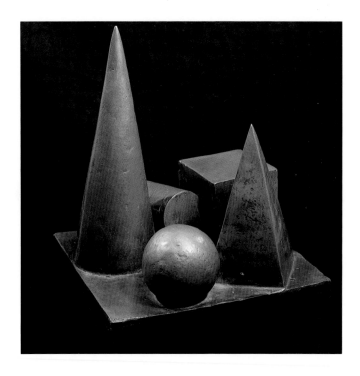

First published in the United States of America in 1989 by
RIZZOLI INTERNATIONAL PUBLICATIONS, INC.
300 Park Avenue South
New York, NY 10010

Library of Congress Catalog Card Number 89-045433
ISBN 0-8478-1151-4 Hardbound
ISBN 0-8478-1126-3 Softbound

Translated from the German by
Thomas Rainer Fischer and Christina Rathgeber
Designed by Kim Shkapich
Printed and bound in Japan.

THE SEVEN COLUMNS OF ARCHITECTURE

THE GEOMETRY

DIE GEOMETRIE

Vorgedrungen
an den Strand der Ägäis
noch in den Schultern
die fruchtbare Feuchtigkeit des Waldes
sah
Archaeus die Zeichen
mit Stab und Schnur
in den Sand geschrieben
bald unkenntlich
im Rhythmus der Wellen
zerronnen.
Doch blieb sein Auge geschärft
und sein Schritt gemessen
beim Gang
durch die Häuser, Städte und Tempel
Regel und Maß.

Having reached
the Aegean Shore
on his shoulders still
the fertile dampness of the forest
Archaeus saw
the signs
written with stick and string
into the sand
soon indecipherable
fading
with the rhythm of the waves.
But his eyes remained sharpened
and his step even
as he walked
through the houses, cities and temples
Rule and Measure.

THE CONSTRUCTION

DIE KONSTRUKTION

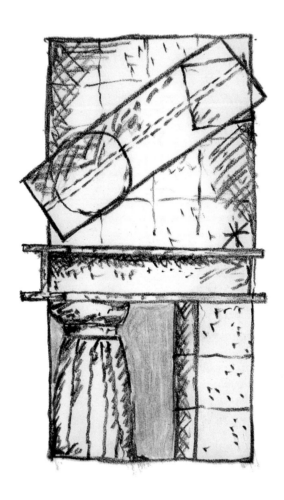

So
hat er die Stufen
die Last verspürt
im Sonnenlicht
gleißend
die Balken
die Pfeiler im Gleichmaß des Steines
Tod und Ewigkeit
statisch und fortschreitend der Fuß
der Bügel
schon über den Wolken.

So
he sensed
the steps, the burden
in the sunlight
glistening
the beams
the pillars in the evenness of stone
death and eternity
static and progressing the foot
the Hanger
already over the Clouds.

THE HARMONY

DIE HARMONIE

Die Sinne fröhlich
erwartungsvoll
schritt er fort mit Pythagoras in
die Harmonie der Sphären
mit sieben Planeten
das zentrale Feuer umkreisend
Mensch im Kreis
Leib — Seele
dem Ohr verborgen die sieben Saiten
des Heptachords.
Iktinos aber *sah*
den Gleichklang der Teile als Ganzes
das sinnliche Scheinen der Idee
im Auge
Licht und Schatten.

Blithe of spirit
expectant
he entered with Pythagoras into
the harmony of the spheres
with seven planets
orbiting the central fire
man in the circle
body - soul
hidden to the ear the seven strings
of the heptachord
but Ictinus *saw*
the parts in accord as a whole
the perceptible manifestation of the idea
in the eye
Light and Shadow.

THE PERFECTION

DIE VOLLKOMMENHEIT

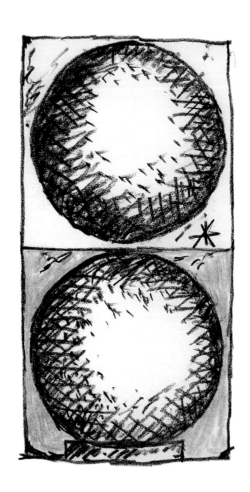

So
tat Archaeus den Schritt
aus dem Gewölbe
aus der Kuppel
heraus in den Kugelraum
die Negation der Bestimmtheit
Einheit
suchend
Eidos und Tyche
im Schwarz des Meeres
Universum der Sterne
über den Ufern der Strekla
Kenotaph und Lebensquell
abstrakte Wirklichkeit
reine Form
mit Archaeus das Kind
der Wilde, der Metaphysiker.

So
Archaeus took the step
out of the vault
out from under the dome
out into spheric space
the negation of certainty
seeking
unity
Eidos and Tyche
in the blackness of the sea
universe of the stars
above the banks of the Strekla
Cenotaph and Fountain of Life
abstract reality
pure form
with Archaeus, the child
the savage, the metaphysician.

THE FUNCTION

DIE FUNKTION

Schon aber
in der Negation der Bestimmtheit
die Revision des *IST* durch das *SEI*
glauben und wissen
ungleicher Schritt
überhöht ins All
noch
cartesianisch verklärt das Gesicht
verkommt
empirisch genötigt
die Hoffnung der Neuzeit
in nützliche Welt
rasend unkundig
verneint sie
Vernunft und Sehnsucht
im Rad der Geschichte.

But already
in the negation of certainty
the revision of IS by TO BE
believing and knowing
uneven step
transcending into space
the face
still
transfigured in Cartesian radiance
empirically compelled
the hope of the new age
decays
in a utilitarian world
furious incognizance
denying
reason and longing
in the wheel of history.

THE UTOPIA

DIE UTOPIE

Spiralig
geschraubt in ferne Welten
böses Träumen
reines Hoffen
Babel und Utopia
der unsichtbaren Städte Glück und Leid
ou
topos
Nichtort
Niemandsland
Engel der Geschichte
Noro lim und Asfaloth
Sonnenstaat und Bienenfabel
mich aber
Thomas
lehrst *Du* nicht
Morus.

Spiralling
into far-off worlds
evil dreams
pure hope
Babel and Utopia
the invisible cities' sorrow and joy
ou
topos
No Place
No Man's Land
Angel of History
Noro Lim and Asfaloth
Sun State and Fable of the Bees
but me
Thomas
You will not teach
More.

THE POETRY

DIE POESIE

So
am Fuße der Neuzeit
an den Anfang
den Punkt des Lebens zurückgekehrt
grüßt
hoch über den Wurzeln des Regens er
vom Gipfel des Chimborazo
winkt Archaeus
hinweg über Welten
an die alten Ufer
und hinauf an den Äther
entdeckt er
im Modul des Fluges das Leben:
poesia quia regulae.

So
at the foot of the new age
having returned to the beginning
to life's first point
He greets
high above the roots of rain
from the peak of Chimborazo
Archaeus waves
over and above worlds
to the old shores
and up towards the ether
he discovers
life in the module of flight:
poesia quia regulae.

ACKNOWLEGEMENTS

When people speak of *The Cooper Union,* whether in Tokyo or in Berlin, they generally mean the *Irwin S. Chanin School of Architecture.* Its Dean, professor John Hejduk, has directed the school for many years and has guided it to international acclaim through the creative efforts of its faculty and students. For me, it is a great honor and pleasure to be asked to exhibit selections of my work at The Cooper Union.

This publication on the occasion of the exhibition presents my museum projects, but the drawings and projects in the book are not necessarily identical with those in the exhibition. Of the five projects presently under construction, particular mention is given to the Pre-history Museum in Frankfurt as a representative example of my work.

I must thank The Cooper Union for the Advancement of Science and Art and its new president John Jay Iselin for his support of the exhibition and publication.

I wish to thank Gianfranco Monacelli of Rizzoli International Publications for his encouragement.

I owe my gratitude and admiration to Kim Shkapich, who created and at the same time controlled, the design of this book, page by page. My thanks to Hélène Binet for the magnificent photography of the Pre-history Museum, she captured an angle of vision, that caught an essence of the spirit of place.

I must thank Dr. Claus Baldus of Berlin for his participation and insights.

I want to thank John Hejduk for the initiation of the exhibition and the publication, and for their realization. Above all, I thank him for the friendship that has held us together for many years.

Josef P. Kleihues
May 1989

Embedded in its charter and emblazoned on its Foundation Building is Cooper Union's embracing goal: promoting knowledge through the advancement of science and art. Publishing this major architectural work signifies the validity of that educational quest.

This volume of extraordinary museum designs accompanies the first exhibition in the United States by an internationally renowned architect, Josef Paul Kleihues. Currently Irwin S. Chanin Distinguished International Professor, Josef Paul Kleihues, through his life work, exemplifies Cooper Union's aspiration for the creative conjunction of technology and artistry.

In truth, the act of publishing meritorious material requires a fruitful union of science and art. In that realization, publishing has enriched immensely the cultural life of our age. Vital ideas are as near at hand as the closest bookstore, newsstand or, on occasion, television set.

Publishing's advancement of public knowledge in the twentieth century however, has been uneven. One substantial cultural calling, embodying somewhat ironically the nexus of engineering and design, has attracted too little quality publishing. That field is architecture itself.

This publication helps offset that unwarranted and inexplicable oversight. In its sponsorship of the exhibition of the museum work of Josef Paul Kleihues, Cooper Union also attests to its own intention to assist public understanding of distinctive design.

As this century nears its close, the cultural challenge is no longer access to ideas. In an age of information abundance, the pressing urgency is for the mastery of knowledge. In this respect, architecture excels in demonstrating the human dimension of soaring ideas.

Within the field of architecture, itself, museums inherently invite bold and compelling concepts. Many building projects inevitably circumscribe the architect's imagination. But major museums should mirror and enhance cultural connections. At their best, they are spaces that expand the mind and ennoble the spirit.

To this global design challenge, Josef Paul Kleihues has applied his exceptional skill. He has, again and again, returned to the qualities of form and the educational function of the museum. The extraordinary results are encompassed in this "Museum" exhibition at The Cooper Union. They are also richly reflected in this book.

Through his enlightened professionalism, in practice and in teaching, Josef Paul Kleihues has established himself as a celebrated citizen of the world.

John Jay Iselin

JOSEF PAUL KLEIHUES:
ARCHITECT OF THE ABANDONED SOUNDS

There is the short distance runner architect and there is the long distance runner architect. Josef Kleihues is a long distance runner. I like and prefer him for this and for his objectives. I respect him for his determination, for his focus, for his precision, his stamina / tenacity, for his stoicism, for his creative energy, for his impeccable understanding of good form, and for his achievements. This long distance runner gets better with age, his distance is extended; his architecture at once becomes sparser and richer. He captures the long abandoned sounds of architecture. He celebrates the ancient laws and mysteries of the rites of construction. He brings forth through his knowledge of materials and detail the density of brooding stone, the dark soul of steel, the thought/reflection of glass, the ecclesiasticalness of wood, the softness of earth and the crystallization of air. He is the architect of pewter. He polishes architecture with the palm of his hand and places it in a landscape with the care that the painter Giorgio Morandi gave to his still lifes.

The short distance runner is just that, a short distance runner. His trail is straight, flat, and the end can be seen. He is a crowd pleaser. He runs fast and is soon out of breath. The long distance runner's scope is simply vaster. He transverses a more complex landscape. He is aware of the changing ground plane beneath him, its hardness and its softness. He feels the topographic elevational differences. He is in it for the long run. He paces himself. Earth, trees, rocks, plants, and water are his markers. He has the time to sense the nuances of the pressure of the atmosphere and of the changing qualities of light. He measures the distances through the pounding of his heart. He is in communion.

Josef Kleihues is an architect that addresses through building the social issues of our time. Hospitals, sanitation, housing, and museums are the programs that call for his attention. The hospital and the museum are not so distant cousins. The hospital attempts to heal the body; the museum attempts to heal the soul.

There is a rehabilitation pool in Kleihues' Berlin Hospital. A pool which exudes the aura and very essence of liquid. Staring into the pool I could not help but be reminded of that rare moment in Jean Cocteau's film: Orphee: where Eurydice and Death move through a rooms' mirror into the *other world*. They moved through a reflection which had the density and consistency of mercury. Josef Kleihues' room/pool bathes the heat of fever and the devastation of disease. His room/pool confronts the opacities of reflections. He insists on the sacredness of materials to ease pain, and to permit ascent. The Berlin Hospital's room/pool is the body's chapel and his Frankfurt Museum is the soul's chapel. In Berlin the agonies of the body are housed and comforted; in Frankfurt the questions of the mind are housed and projected. In Berlin light is let in; in Frankfurt warmth is let in. In Berlin the hospital's function is for the body;

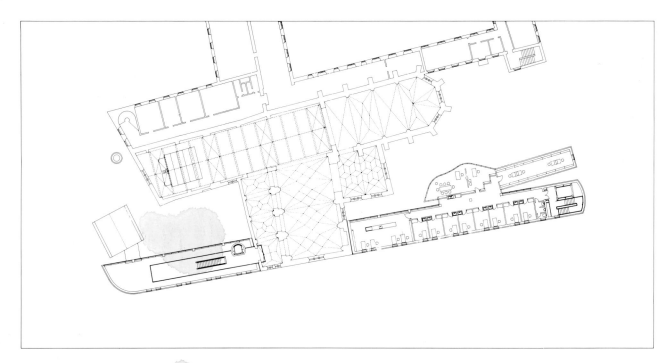

in Frankfurt the museum's function is for the spirit. When one grasps a handrail in Berlin it is for physical support; when one grasps a handrail in Frankfurt it is for moral support. In Berlin man is cared for, in Frankfurt God is spoken to. The lips move but no sound is emitted, for it is absorbed within. There is a *within* speaking.

Museums are the receptacles of lost sounds. Museums are the sarcophagi of past thoughts and are the covenants with sacred cultures. Museums were meant as havens for the solitary travellers. In their times they functioned as the guardians to loninesess. They protected the soul. There are few left that do so today and there are hardly any that are created anew. The Frankfurt Museum of Josef Kleihues *is* such a place. I have often said that to be a master of architecture one has to do a single masterwork, with the completion of the Frankfurt Museum, Josef Kleihues can be considered so.

The architect has the responsibility and obligation to whisper to space and to gently fondle its audial volumes. He must fall in love with its voidness. He should blow soft kisses to architecture's silence. He has the strength to inhale the delicious space of fog into his heart. He is able to caress with his fingers the velvetness of dark marbles and knows the immense joy of embracing the thoughts of architecture. The architect knows the aromas of life and death. The architect smells the juices of wood. His skin tingles at the touch of granite. A nail sunk into pine is a nail entombed. Steel always brings forth the name blacksmith. Fire makes hard. There are few sounds that awaken the bats of hell. The sound of a steel hammer banging upon a steel beam makes them screech. The drying of plaster echoes the cold dampness of the recently buried. Architecture is the precise approximate.

I will address two aspects of Josef Kleihues' Museum of Pre- and Early History in Frankfurt, they are the plan and the new steel structure spanning the old church.

One is struck by the fact that the plan appears (when seen as vertical section) to be some kind of phantom ship carrying a sacred cargo. And so it does. The plan protects the necessity of the new or of youth taking good care of the old or aged. The new plan of the museum is like a swift computerized low slung vessel plying the rivers of Germany announcing its intent to protect ancient structures and to celebrate, in this particular case it carries as its consigned cargo the old structure of the church. In plan the old church's roof ribbings seem to act as rope nettings supporting the contents of past times, with the addition of new steel cables holding in place the container of long ago sorrows. A delicate equilibrium is achieved, the voices singing a hymn within the darkened hall produce the necessary volume of air preventing collapse. The funereal husks of the River Nile, the barges of Hamburg and the death launches of Venice come to mind. The prow of this museum river ship cuts through the water as a surgeon's knife cuts through the skin. The plan must be looked upon as a vertical section and then we see at the prow the tilted cube observing the progress of the operation. The secular and the sacred are welded together for a brief moment. We even can imagine that the old church has lifted the new ship above the surface of the water and it is floating in air at an acute angle. It is the architects obligation to see things momentarily this way, his disipline requires this to be so.

For an architect looking at x-rays showing the metal connectors joining and replacing bones is a strange sobering experience. The bones are connected by new metal/steel structures that have a ghostly beauty. They remind one of the Maillart/Morandi concrete structures but fabricated in steel, miniaturized, then placed in deep charcoal grey waters. They are like sea urchins made of polished metal brought to a dull finish.

The steel roof structure spanning the great hall in the Frankfurt Museum is as the above. A unique, organic structure is installed. A perfect integration of the old and of the new. One is aware that something profound has occurred. A healing has taken place. Kleihues' bridging is elegant and eloquent. And the way it is detailed has no equivalent. This roof structure is uncanny as it is eerie, it has been able to conjour up the sense of the past. But at the same time is an impregnating modern. It is like being in a three dimensional x-ray. It is as our internal bodies are. The skin adapting to the movement of blood and water so that the soul can remain free.

The Hospital and the Museum are co-joined through the thoughts of an architect.

My friend Josef has many physicians within his family and most likely would prefer not to be called a medicine man. But I think he is; in the best interpretation. That is before the advent of modern science, perhaps in pre-history times there were those who administered to the concerns of the soul with the hope of healing the body and in a way they were architects before the name architect came into being.

March 1989
John Hejduk

39

CONCEPT AND PRACTICE OF MEMORY, ALTERNATING TYPOLOGY OF ABSTRACT ESTHETICAL FORM

Dialogue:

Dr. Claus Baldus

and

Josef P. Kleihues

B.

Museums deal with history, but also primarily with memory. Let's discuss the term *anamnesis.* It is slightly changed from the original when translated to mean *remembering.* It actually means *not forgetting.* Anamnesis has governed classical tradition, explicitly since Plato, and disregarding any historical resonances, up until Hegel. Does the architecture of museums in any way stand in conjunction with the theatrical recurrence of the traditional, by way of postmodernism?

K.

Independent of what the key word *postmodernism* expresses, it generally has a very graphic and illustrative meaning that can be defined as directed theatrical history; this is not only in architecture. In addition, there exists a critical appeal, postmodern or not, that we can probably comprehend better. It deals with memory of *forgotten* or *ignored values*. This is demonstrated, for example, in our understanding of nature, and of the discussion of what is compatible with our environment and of what leads to its destruction.
I'd prefer not to discuss postmodernism, however, but engage in a discussion about memory; it expresses a great deal with regard to the institution of museums, and also applies to my work as an architect in general.

B.

Do you also mean this in respect to the current interest in museums and their structures?

K.

The concept and practice of memory plays a strong part in our understanding of museums as places of collecting and preserving, of classification and presentation. There is also an historical consciousness which exists that is affected both intellectually and emotionally for society in general. And therewithin the concept and practice of memory plays a very important part.

The willingness to remember and the ability to remember what once existed implies an interest in what could or should exist in the future. The concept of memory is originally dependent on the relationship between the rational and historical, with the prerequisite of the rational being independence.

B.

The past, either actual perceived experiences or a collection of reports, descriptions, and narrations of time gone by, is, according to Nietzsche and Freud, more than just recollective activity; it is *spontaneous or perhaps even unconsciously experienced repetition.* The past is *precautious; it is content securing memory,* and a *critical review* of tradition, perhaps with the result of a *liberating detachment* from its consolidation, its restraints, and its coherence of repression. How can these levels of our historically understood existence be brought into coherence with the subject of building for museums?

K.

What you call our historically understood existence for me includes not only interest but also an active support of development for the future. And it's especially this, that I emphasize when I talk of implied orientation toward the future through memory. The German philosopher Adorno, who repeatedly dwells on the question of tradition, discusses the same thing when he comments, "A question doesn't exist that could be asked in which knowledge of the past is not kept, and which doesn't press on ahead to the future."

We must accept that the willingness and ability to remember is always selectively directed, either consciously or subconsciously. This is due to individual

motivation and to individual perception of life in general. The coherence of your assumption of "three levels of our historically understood existence" can be just as inseparable as a comment about their typologies.

B.

Can you elaborate on this by using examples of your own work?

K.

I've observed in my method of design that during the first graphic or conceptual approach to a project, an abstract geometrical form develops, more as a *subject* of design than as a *prototype.*

Perhaps there's a connection of this with "content securing memory." Geometry identifies the abstract and material, with an alternating evolution of architecture as an object and shape.

I've never been interested in a "liberation" of tradition; currently demonstrated, for example, in the recent tendency of destructive manipulation of genetics. However, a poetical relativity of geometrical stringence is certainly allowed. There is a type of uniformity in design demonstrated by projects such as the exhibition pavilion for Documenta 6 in Kassel in 1977, the museums in Blankenheim, Sindelfingen, and Kornwestheim, the Museum of the Three Geometrical Rooms for Documenta 8 in 1988, the program for reuse of the former flower market halls in Hamburg, as well as the Groningen project. A geometrical image is spontaneously transcribed within the required environmental and historical situation.

B.

Isn't the current revival of museums in Germany connected to the historicization of vocabulary and the spacial conception of modernism? The modern, analytical, simplifying, and reductive intent of design currently overplays itself: "superior determination," to use terminology from the metaphysics of Freud. There is a second layer, a sphere of historical insinuations that covers the syntax of functionalism, constructivism, dadaism, and other paradigms that have taken the risk of breaking with tradition. In which way does repeated memory of history stand together with a

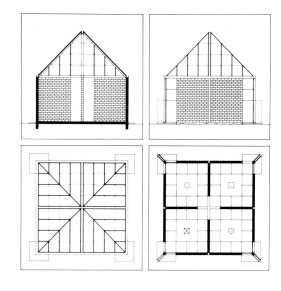

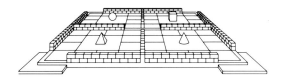

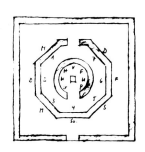

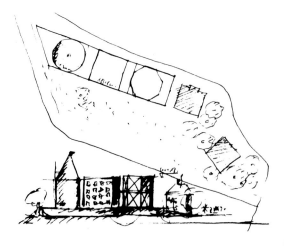

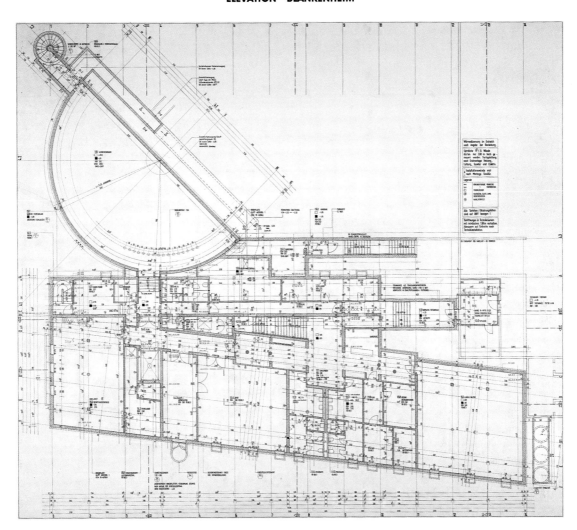

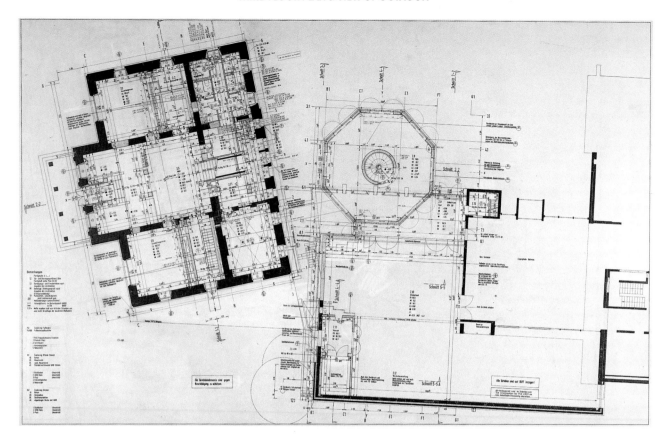

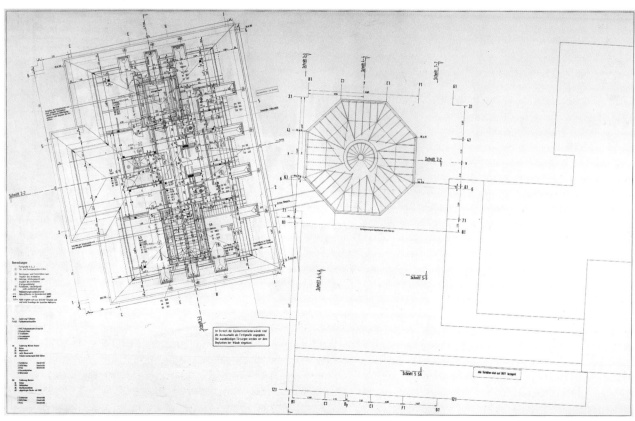

revival of the rhetorical, tropia of vocabular architecture, and the contextualization   of   urban
space and structural geometry?

K.

**I haven't dealt closely with the metaphysics of Freud,
and so I can't respond to your comment on this. When
you talk of the "realm of historical connotations" in
present day architecture, there certainly are a number
of examples. We must differentiate between the pre-
posed acquisition and playful application of such historically connotated images and valid theoretical
and architectural experimentation.**

**A design for a museum is perhaps a special chal-
lenge for experimentation, although it still remains a
project with very specific requirements. Because of
this, I can't understand why some architects tend to
think that museum projects open the door to an unlim-
ited "design exercise."**

**Regardless of the different positions in architectural
theory, it isn't the type of a project but the path to its
materialization that defines the extent of freedom
used in the design process. Freedom in design isn't
defined by quantity, but by quality. Who can determine
a greater amount of freedom than that taken in the
design for the New National Gallery in Berlin by Mies
van der Rohe, or for the State Library, also in Berlin by
Hans Scharoun? And what would be the point of such a
determination? What does interest us, however, is the
differentiated direction of *freedom of design,* and the
respective *alternating typology of abstract esthetical
form* as a result of different memories and their various
utilizations.**

B.

And as in the philosophical or critical usage of
memory, based on a type of enlightenment!

If I recall your earlier museum projects, the
Sprengelmuseum in Hannover and the Landes-
galerie in Düsseldorf, it seems that these works
present themselves as narrated memories.

K.

**You correctly refer to the narrative character of these
two projects, which was a result of the intention to
transfer images and paintings (Baselitz, Lüpertz, Malevich) into the language of architecture. This is obvious**

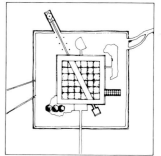

in the drawings of the houses for my friends, the painters Baselitz and Lüpertz, which were created at the same time as the design of the Sprengelmuseum. These projects were informative experiments with respect to the affinity between painting, sculpture, and architecture, and exposed at the same time the divergence in their possible expression. The results are still a part of my thoughts; as much as we discuss architecture theoretically, it can't be explained by the rational alone because it is inseparable from imagery.

You'll discover narrative elements of imagery in my newest projects and in future works. But as I've already said, my main point of interest is in identity through scale and proportion in the context of geometrical rules, in the sense of a mediator between the abstract and material. This concerns aspects of continuity, which develop into geometrical form, including cleavages and discordances.

Geometry has a type of categorical purpose in relation to time and space. For example: think of the simple monotacticle sequence of columns in Apameia (Syria): static and in stone, they imply direction and time.

The monotacticle sequence that refers to time and space, in my opinion, is not part of the classical desire for complete and conclusive systems. The classical desire for complete and uniform systems (i.e. rhythmical systems) is achieved easier through paratacticle or other types of sequences. Sequences and other geometrical systems of reference, are applied dialectically; such duplications are a basic element of classical dialectics.

B.

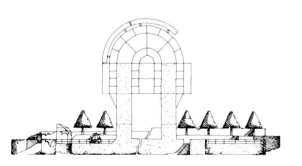

Let's discuss for a moment the principle of duplication. As a basic element of classical dialectics, in a modern interpretation, it combines itself with an infinitely long chain of strategic maneuvers of seriality or aleatorics, of displacements, superimpositions, or transformations that all have one thing in common: they can't be kept in a final synthesis. Differentiation, openness, and liberation mean more than the superficially remaining commitment to pluralism. Not until we lose the compulsion to systematize, questioned by Kierkegaard and Nietzsche, so that systematic thinking consciously possesses tentative, preliminary, and experimental character, can alternative paradigms legitimately exist, competing and corresponding with each other. The resulting maintenance of pluralism by acquisition of a syntax for duplication is, in modern terms, an acquisition of divergence, and the toleration thereof. This concerns not only architecture presently but is an informative analogy for philosophy, anthropology, and other cultural fields.

Wasn't the principle of duplication used not only in your project in Frankfurt but also in Sindelfingen and Solingen? The dialectical proportion that exists in these designs is varied but strongly accentuated by the historical structural elements that you had to respect or integrate.

K.

What you call the syntax or the principle of duplication and its dialectical purposes is a product of time and space. We encounter it in the correlation of the traditional and modern. These relationships, however, are losing validity, as the one has quality whereas the other one doesn't. Therefore, there can't be any discussion of competing or corresponding paradigms.

The affinity of the Gothic City Hall in Munster to the Renaissance facade of the Stadtweinhaus (Civic Wine Authority) standing next to it is considered exceptional. This type of affirmation is directly, perhaps *too* directly, demonstrated by O.M. Ungers in Karlsruhe when he projected the profile of the Church of St. Stephan's by Weinbrenner onto the side of his library standing across from it.

It is the competing paradigm in Santiago de Compostela of voluminous monasteries, churches, and palaces next to the conglomeration of small-unit housing which gives this historical urban monument the same impression that was accomplished by Josef Schattner in Eichstatt, though in a much more subtle manner. The new construction done for the IBA (International Building Exhibition of 1987 in Berlin), built under the context of the "critical reconstruction of the city," is probably the most complex urban example of corresponding and competing paradigms.

As far as this concerns the Frankfurt, Sindelfingen & Solingen museum projects, there was a direct challenge created by the different structural histories in all three places.

In Frankfurt this is demonstrated by the special affinity of modern buildings to the Gothic Carmelite Church, and also of the former Carmelite Monastery in context to the historical city.

The baroque Gräfrather Monastery and the building complex on top of the monastery hill had a completely

different potential for *memory*. The project in Sindelfingen was challenged by the bourgeois-classical purism of the former Town Hall.

These three examples, mentioned in your question, possibly are each so distinct that they distract from my general interest of an analytical discourse with history. This is an experimental application of abstract design, which experienced a breakthrough in the 1920s, having developed in a theoretical and technically diverse modulation. Design projects that have developed in the same way are manifested basically in the theoretical concept, and then in the subjects of architectural imagery. Finally, they are substantiated by the choice of materials, and of structural detailing. For the "alternating typology" in my work it is important that the rules of geometry, and of proportion and scale, have greater input than just simple coincidence; the abstract architectural *form* enables a much more legible statement than the architectural shape, so avowed by others. It is important that the choice of materials has priority over the choice of color and that there is no alternative to well-crafted and structurally sound detailing.

B.

That commitment, at least in its tendency, assures a greater interest in historical continuity than in a severance.

K.

It's a question of definition. We shouldn't overlook the fact that architectural modernism (Mies van der Rohe & Le Corbusier, Gropius & Scharoun) supports this severance. In the end, however, modernism has developed and cultivated in a *new way* its vocabulary out of that which at one time existed. I don't want to evade your question with this answer, but rather admit that with all my enthusiasm for risking and experimenting —the satisfaction of work alone produces curiosity— I'm not so interested in what can be done as in what is required; and in respect to the particular situation, what it's worth to have it materialize.

I know the *ecstasy of creativity* quite well, but I also know its dangers. An ecstasy of creating, producing, and consuming obviously exists, not only in technology and in economy but also in culture. Recently creativity in architecture shows a type of alienated ecstasy of work that is exhausted in a "rage of originality" ('Originalitätswuth' — Nietzsche) by an addictive yearning for "new creations."

B.

Is it constant work on closely defined subjects that you use to work against that? Proportions, scale, geometry? What does the use of the primary shapes in architecture mean to you? They permanently reappear, always as new variations, in your work, for example: the semicircle (in Kornwestheim and the hospital in Berlin-Neukölln), the octagon (Sindelfingen), the combination of geometrical rooms (Kassel) or of geometrical objects (Groningen), which are based on the square, the octagon, and the circle.

K.

First I'd like to continue with the "alienated ecstasy of methodology." This form of creating something at all costs is concerned with materialization more than with production; often not just for economical or technical reasons, but because it is socially legitimate.

To discuss further the development of modernist design, there are rational sources that are of great interest to me: aspects of geometry, the concepts of abstraction, transparency, light space, and time. Geometrical shapes have an unreasonable immaterial typology, as does the perception of time and/or space. It is exactly because of this that mediation of the abstract and material is of great interest; they are applied in design by use of geometrical shapes, elements, and structures, because within this there is a general applicable "syntax," which allows for extremely different expressions.

Measure and scale, for instance, or rather what we call modular organization, was used by Blondell, Durand, Le Corbusier, and Mies van der Rohe with very curious, theoretical purposes and artistic conceptions. If we accept the fact that ever since the enlightenment an increasing number of different analytical theories have existed (an attempt to define them was made in 1984 in the exhibition "Adventure of Ideas," subtitled "Architecture and Philosophy," in the New National Gallery of Berlin), then we can justly prove the desire, destain, and variation of the usage of modular organization in respect to the once defined "theoretical structure" of architecture and its historical development.

Regardless of the common genealogical roots of classicism and rationalism, we can confirm that classicism has a tendency to be directed with greater stabilization towards determination which perhaps defends new experiences and perceptions with great-

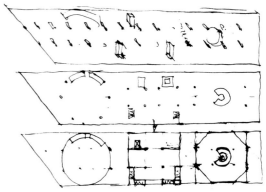

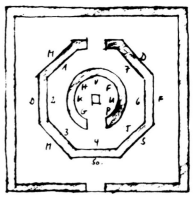

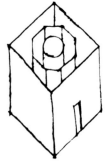

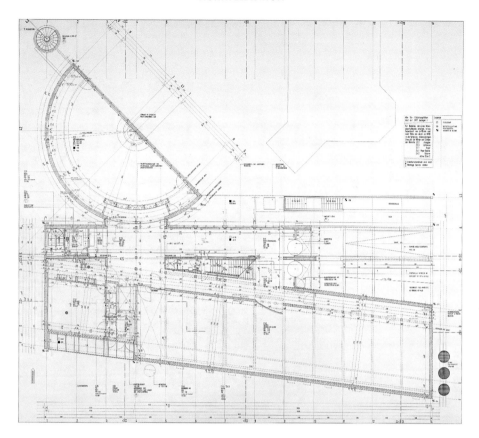

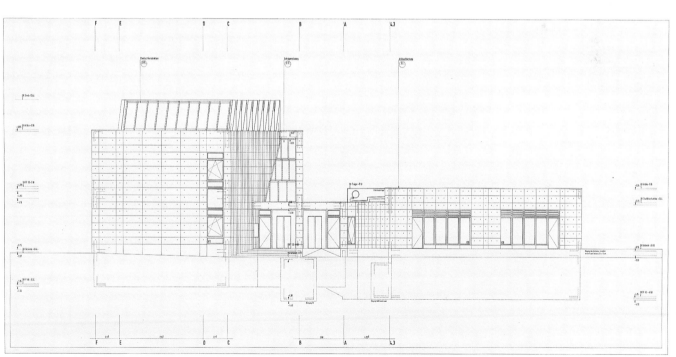

DETAILS OF OCTAGON STEEL CONSTRUCTION
SINDELFINGEN

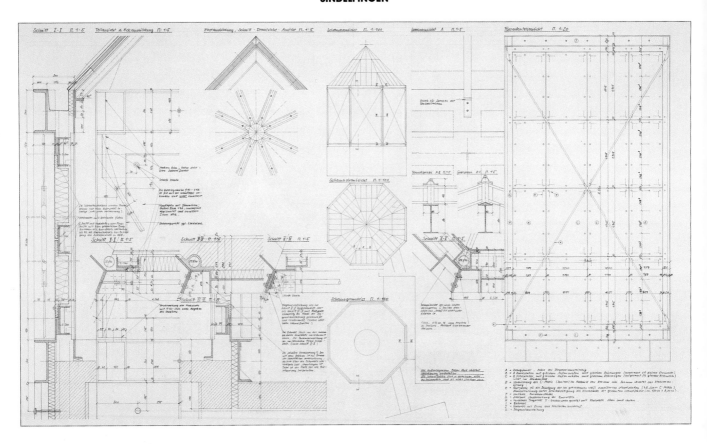

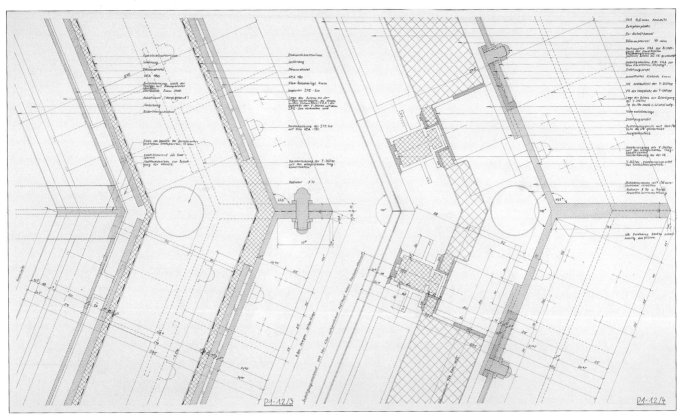

52

er logic. It is odd that both theories use modular and geometrical orders.

B.

Can you articulate this hypothesis?

K.

In classically directed design, geometry and proportions stand for harmony, solidity, cosmology, truth, esthetic purity, and perhaps even absolute perfection. Rationalism, on the other hand, stands for systematics, methodology, mechanics, technology, causality, functionality, economics, and logic. The concept of architecture is expressed in a diversified usage of the same syntax.

B.

Nietzsche's second essay, titled "Purpose and Disadvantages of History for Life in General," published in *Untimely Meditations* in 1874 isn't the only discourse that supported the modern severance with tradition, but for our discussion it is an important text. What is history? Certainly not just an inventory of what once existed, from which we select suitable inspiration according to our desires and aspirations. This very popular conception is too innocent, and obscures the fact that history has an important purpose in the constitution of life.

What is history? Perhaps we can agree to the interpretation in the hermeneutical philosophies of Nietzsche, Dilthey, and Simmel that it is a time chain, which in every living moment takes the future and puts it into the past, a metamorphosis of coming and going, a fleeting threshold of the present that provides for a transition, allowing subjective motivation to coagulate into objective form. It is a suspension of the future. Subjective interest, once produced and presented in material form, becomes objective fact. This transition creates an alienation from enthusiasm, from the spontaneous self-appreciation of our will. Out of the abstract form that was an arbitrator, as productive present, the spontaneous self-representation of subjectivity results in an object of historical inventory and becomes an analytical but no longer spontaneous, mental discourse. The present moment of creative self-awareness is at the same time a severance of the motivation that led to materialization. We describe this moment as *pathos* and avoid it with *fear* or we can accept the feeling of its irrepressive ambivalence (tragedy, as Simmel would later comment), as the purpose of our own unresolved *disintegration* with all that belongs to the past. This moment was for Nietzsche the cause to describe a methodology that positions work with disharmony. Nietzsche places the object, "history," as an image made, objective fact, in dependence to the overall constitution of life, in which longing and desires are administered: *the purpose for and disadvantages of living*.

How could Nietzsche's text be of meaning to historical design?

K.

The typology, which you insinuated, could be of help; differentiating between monumental, antique, and critical history. Or, in other words, between ideological, scientifically preserved, and analytically deduced history.

B.

But the three categories of monumental, antique, and critical history don't lead to a "system" anymore, as in Hegel's "Memory." They don't form a "path of levels" for future subjects that lead to themselves, and therefore to a final self-ascertainment, incumbent and totally dependent on determination. It is typical, however, for Hegel and Nietzsche to give the concept of crisis a completely different status. The classic systematist designates crisis as a level of self-awareness, provocating tendencies to the absolute, just temporarily due to its mediating if not servile function. In the philosophy of life, *crisis* is just one of three possibilities of self-interpretation with respect to history. *Freedom of choice* also exists, and in between, the *historical ego*, acting consciously or unconsciously. Therefore momental force, if not to say pressure of a no longer objectively made, but rather by necessary process legitimately made decision is maneuvered towards involvement, with which modernists, as well as with the existentialism of Kierkegaard, have persistently been engaged.

K.

The commitment to tradition was also a yearning for validity, nurtured by anxety and fear. Tradition relies on the principle of finality with stringent conventions.

B.

Let's stay with Nietzsche for the time being. The result of the second essay in *Untimely Meditations* which to me is the most radical of the four essays in series, is for his part aphoristic, because the question of possible transition, or the subjective change-in-position between selectable approaches to history is no longer discussed. Our priorities can change under the impression of the amended necessities of life. Desire can arise to free us from historical idols that have more or less done their jobs very well for a contained period of time, to free us from historical idols, in order to test us experimentally in the other two approaches.

K.

Nietzsche makes us aware of partiality in particular types of history, and indirectly points out the problem of such positional deviation, or even of relative connotations.

B.

Definitely, but without encountering the logic of transition of tentative clarification. This deficiency, this unsatisfied need for clarification, leaves latent (but latency lying in the trials and tribulations of desire) speculative expectations untouched. After all, the end of the universe could be happy for everyone, or an esthetical code of rules is agreed upon universally with good will. *On the Genealogy of Morals,* published in 1887 which evolved out of texts following the *Untimely Meditations,* was the first text to confront explicitly the systematizing obligation of tradition. History, unremitting and unrevealing as it is, exists according to the *Genealogy* so that its interpretation must be constantly renewed by life experiences, and therefore by speculation. Next to the three ideal designated positions of the historical, now comes a variation of interpreted possibilities, which directs life orientated towards the future, opposite to its past. Traditionally held values that guide our activity as objective legitimate units of fixed points are nothing else than tentative interpretations. I'd like to recall Nietzsche's concept of attempt and temptation so that we can understand the reasonable and determining connections, created with subjectively defined values retrospectively, ex post factum. However, we are only able to understand so much as available causative and respectively structural terminology allows.

How strongly is your work influenced by the large number of "pasts"? Of pasts not objectively *given*, but subjectively *interpreted*, of pasts to which Nietzsche draws our attention in the essay "We Scholars," printed in 1884? I've recognized repeated use of singular subjects in your work, but also a striving for distinct individuality of each design.

K.

Repeated use of singular subjects and striving for distinct individuality has nothing to do with a number of, but with just *one* subjective interpretation of the past, not defined to the last detail but as an ongoing "willingness to learn," coupled with the intent to enrich the tradition of rationalism in architecture with a poetical dimension.

Translated from the German by Thomas Rainer Fischer

The concept of *poetic rationalism,* introduced by Josef Paul Kleihues in the 1970s, characterizes both his designs and his interest in architectural theory. In *Seven Columns of Architecture*, first published in 1984, this interest is focused in the recognition: ''poesia quia regulae.''

In the catalog for the Milan Trienniale, 1988 *World Cities and the Future of the Metropoles*, Kleihues presented the idea of poetic rationalism in this schematic diagram.

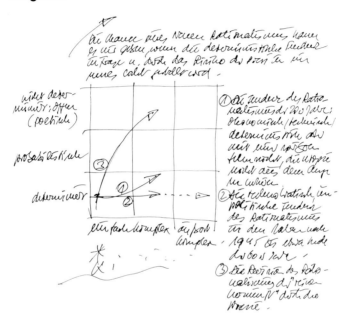

The chance for a new rationalism only exists, if the deterministic tendency is questioned and placed in a new light through the risk of poetry.

not determined: open
(poetic)

probable

determined

simple

complex

extremely complex

1. The tendency of rationalism in the 1920s: economical/technical/deterministic, but with the perceptible yearning not to lose sight of utopia.

2. The technocratic, unpolitical tendency of rationalism in the years after 1945 until roughly the end of the 1960s.

3. The revision of the rationalism of ''pure reason'' through poetry.

SPRENGELMUSEUM

In 1972, more than 180 architects participated in an open competition for the new Sprengelmuseum in Hannover. This marked the beginning of the many subsequent museum projects in the Federal Republic of Germany. It was the first museum competition in which J.P. Kleihues participated.

FRACTURED GALLERY,

REVERSED TUNNEL-FLOWER,

CONCRETE, GLASS AND RIVETED ALUMINIUM

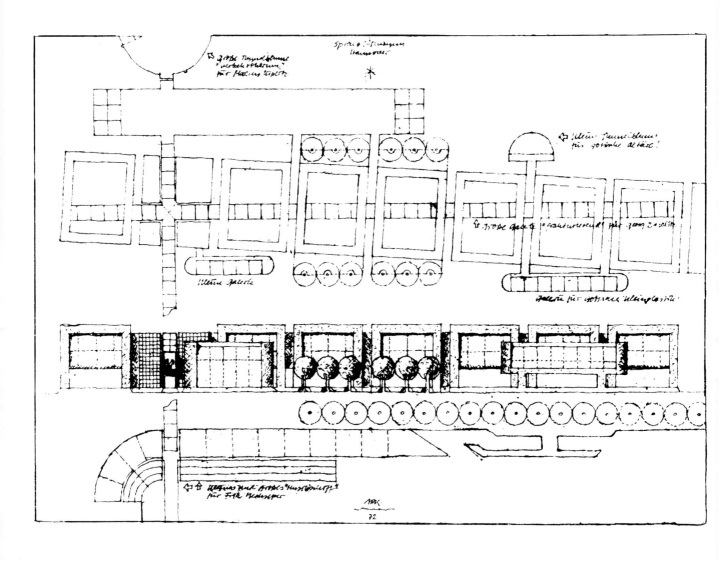

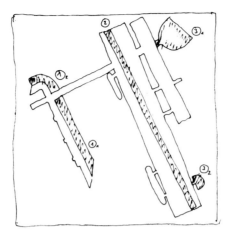

The Sprengelmuseum is composed of primary and attributive elements which have different uses and meanings. Three of these elements are dedicated to friends: the *fractured gallery* to Georg Baselitz; the large reversed *Tunnelblume* (tunnel-flower) to Markus Lüpertz; and the *large and small Musik-Schiff* (music-ship) to Fritz Meckseper.

The assembled row of four-footed exhibition pavilions, 21 meters in height, is found again in a variation in the Düsseldorf Museum. In Hannover a glazed entrance hall forms the intersection between differing units. From here, stairways and ramps lead to suspended exhibition levels. In Düsseldorf, where the museum is more exposed to the urban mechanism, a "fractured Pronaos" is inserted as an entrance element. The building materials of the Sprengelmuseum —concrete, glass and riveted sheet aluminum—determine the color concept.

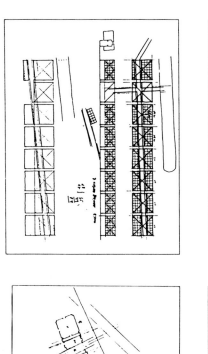
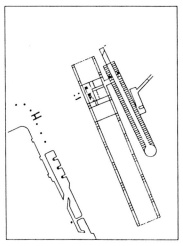
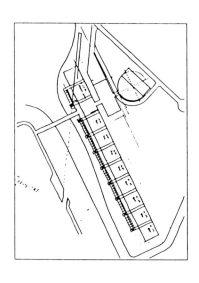
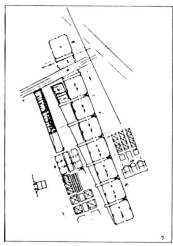
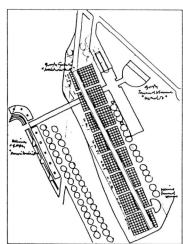
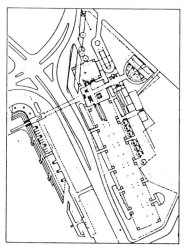

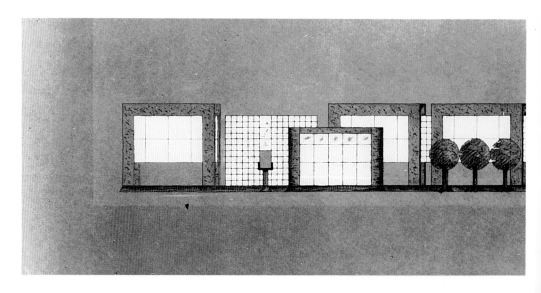

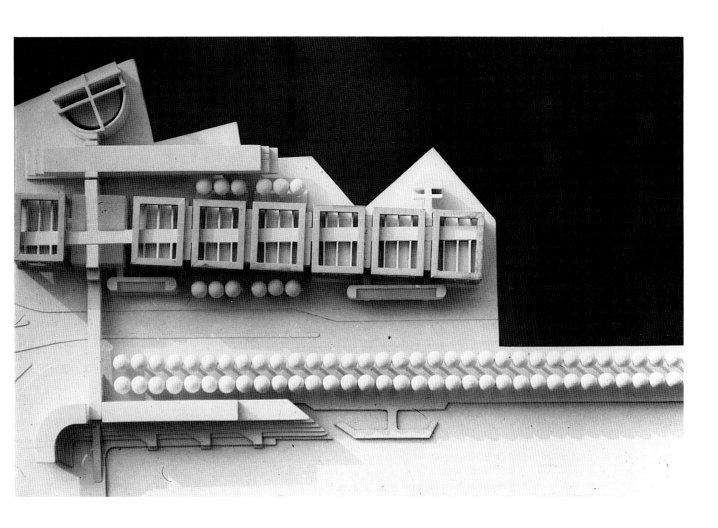

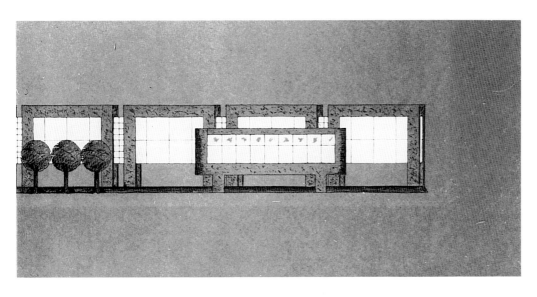

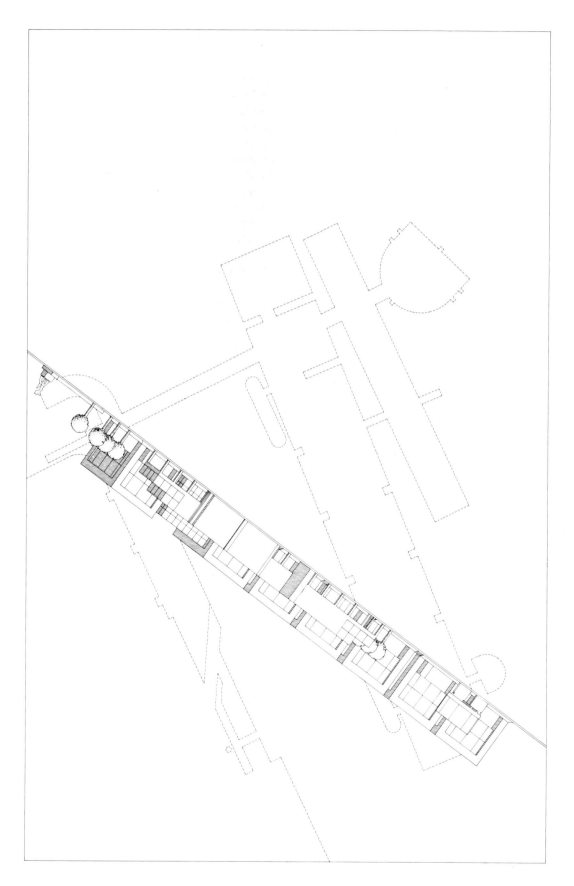

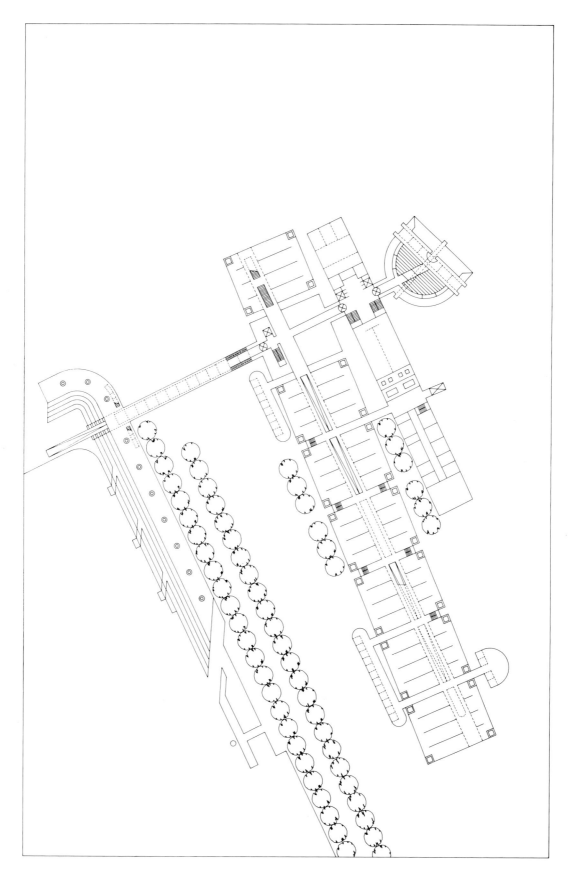

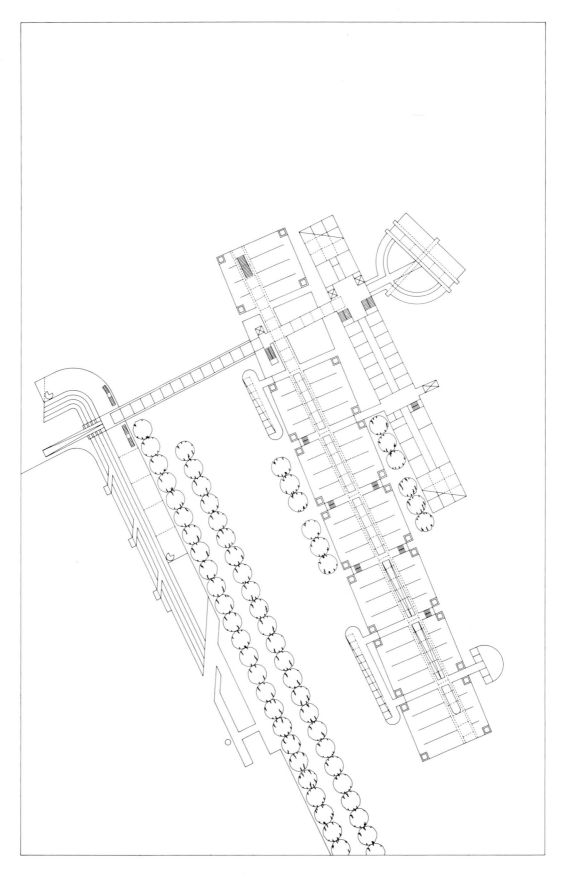

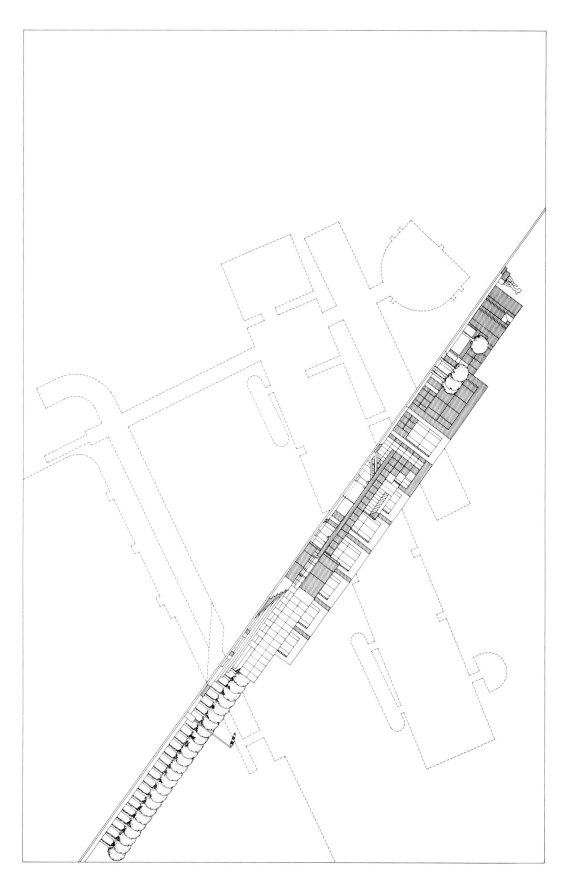

LANDESGALERIE

In 1975 the State of North Rhine-Westphalia announced an open competition for a new building to be the State Art Gallery.

Although not awarded a prize, the competition entry is presented here. The following precis is from the explanatory text submitted to the jury.

FRACTURED PRONAOS

A RED CROSS, and

A CHESTNUT TREE WITH WHITE BLOSSOMS

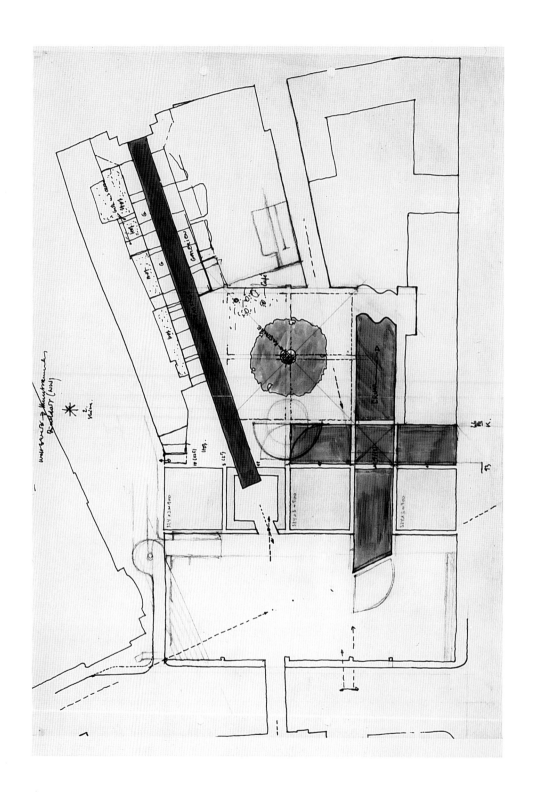

70

Both the selected site for a new building of the State Art Gallery in the heart of the City of Düsseldorf, and the extraordinary high value of the State art collection, were reason enough not only to take the rational and functional needs of a museum into consideration, but also to give cause to define further and greater expectations. The premise of this statement is valid for architecture in general, but it is especially important for public buildings, as a reflection of the cultural and social development of a society. Because of this, solitary structures have an obligation to be an example of that which could be.

The site on the Grabbeplatz marks a meeting point of two worlds: on one side, the irregular narrow, urban structure of the late Middle Ages and on the other side, the strict, classically designed city plan of the 19th Century. The buildings on Grabbeplatz and the understated complexity of the museum courtyards, interlocked into a block system, should be representative of this convergence.

The architectural composition is of just a few elements: the glass gallery *blue,* the exhibition frames *yellow,* the connecting cross *red* and the tree in the center of the museum courtyard, which serves as a passing and meeting point.

The glass gallery in its diagonal path links the rectangular system of the museum to the tangled structure of the old city. It serves simultaneously as a glass covered access to the proposed galleries and studios and as a representative connection to the entrance hall of the museum, symbolized by an open concrete frame.

The exhibition frames are large concrete pavilions set on four legs having different heights of varying forms similar to those designed in 1972 for the Sprengelmuseum in Hannover. They are intended as a poetic gesture to the tradition of classical architecture as well as an homage to Donald Judd. The concrete frame, fractured in the path of the glass gallery, symbolizes the vestibule (Pronaos) of the museum, and simultaneously the connection to the old city and the Grabbeplatz. This fractured "Pronaos" is dedicated to my friend George Baselitz.

The connecting cross links both ordinates of the museum, the defined facade on Grabbeplatz Square and the proposed street facade as an extension to the Court Gardens. It serves as an internal element for orientation and circulation and encloses the most important, purely functional spaces, and is in memory of Kasimir Malevich.

The tree proposed for the courtyard, a chestnut with white blossoms, is planted in the paved square, as a natural focal point between the Old and the New.

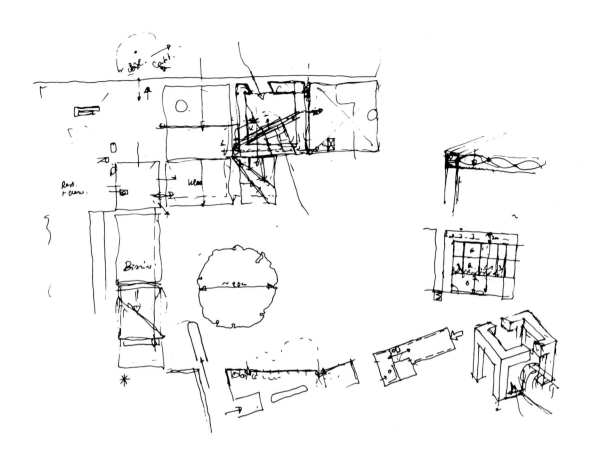

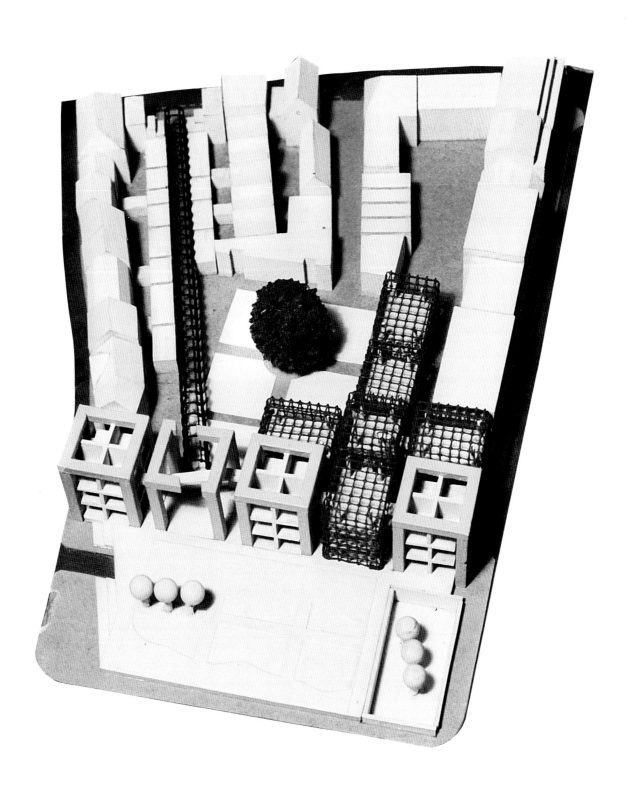

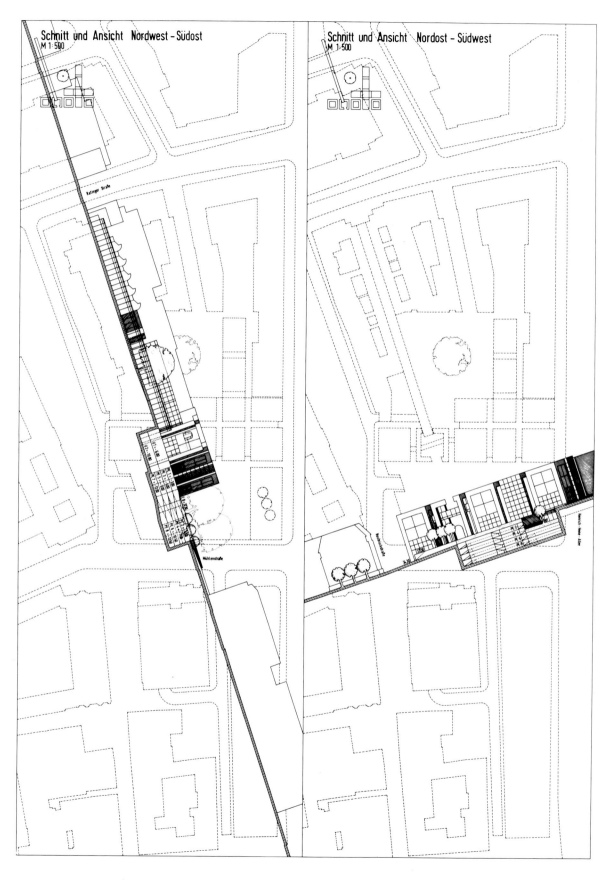

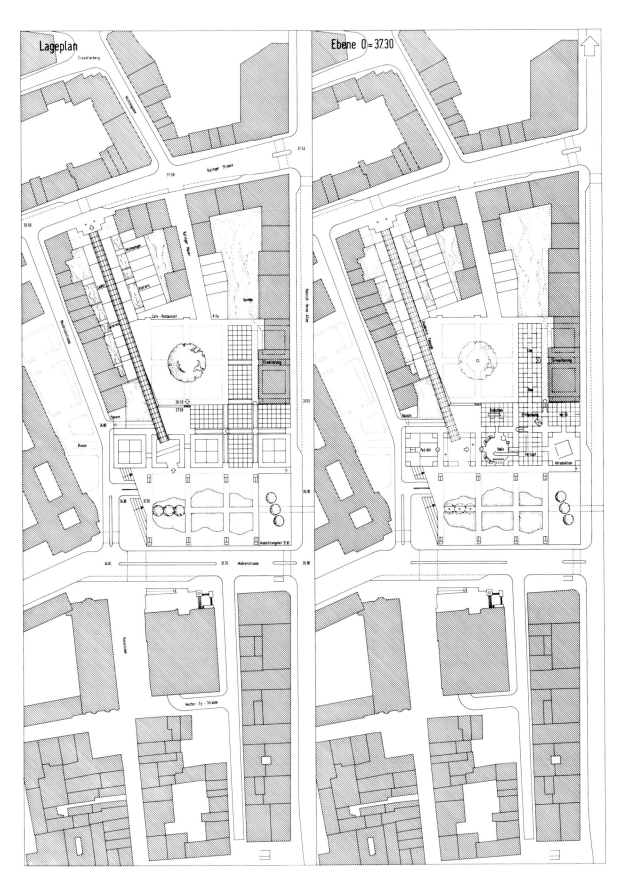

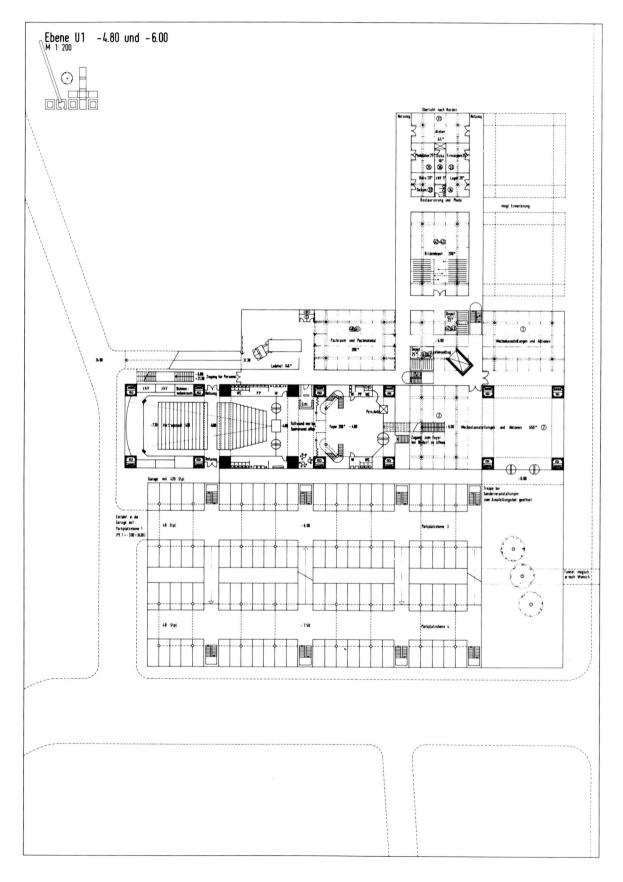

Ebene U1   -4.80 und -6.00
M 1:200

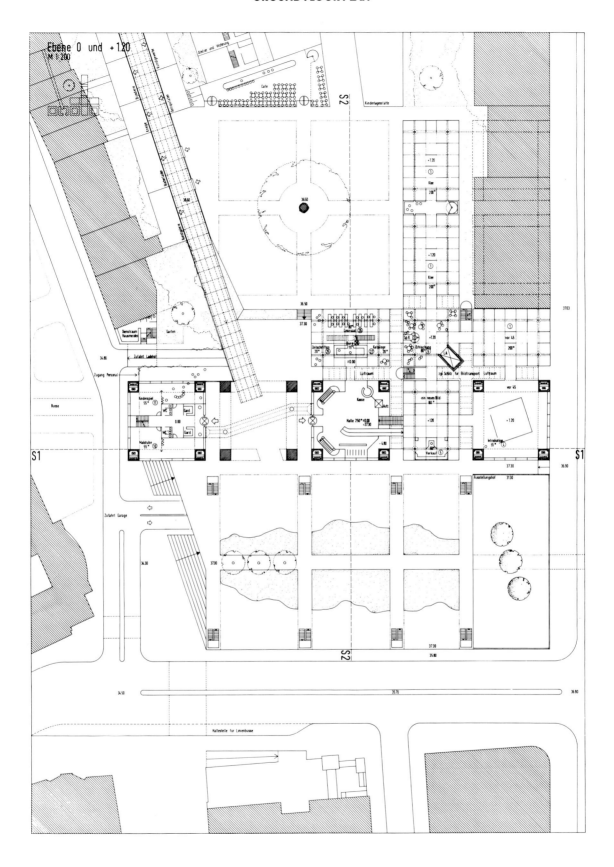

RECONSTRUCTION OF THE PALAIS EPHRAIM AND THE JEWISH MUSEUM

In 1978 four architects were invited to submit proposals for the reconstruction of the former Ephraim Palais and for an extension which would house the Jewish Museum, Berlin. J.P. Kleihues' design was ranked second. None of the submitted designs was ever realized. Instead, some years later the Berlin Senate gave the stones of the former Ephraim Palais, which had been in storage in West Berlin, to East Berlin. This decision was the best possible solution: the Ephraim Palais was reconstructed in the immediate vicinity of its original location. While this documentation was being prepared, an open competition, with special invitations, for the construction of a Jewish museum was announced.

STONES AS MEMORY

THOUGHT AS MEMORY

"HISTORY'S MARK ON THINGS, WORDS, COLORS AND TONES..."

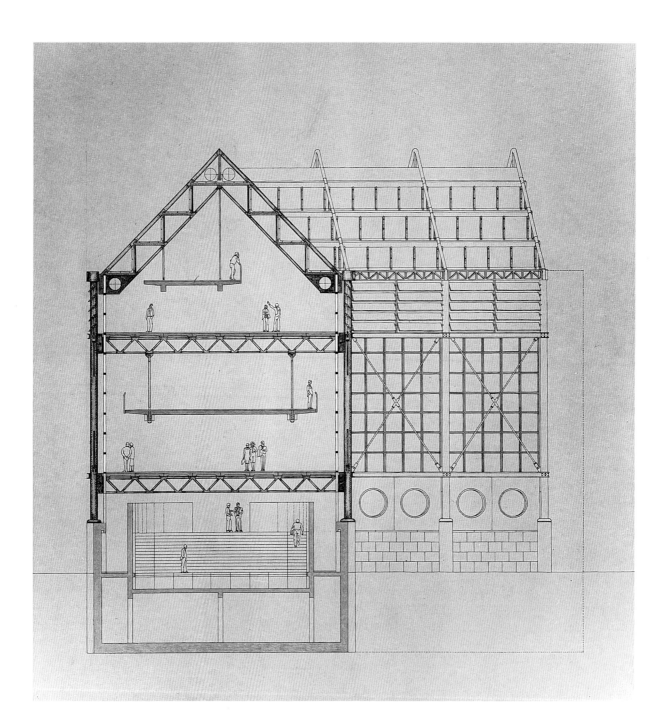

Until the widening of the Mühlendamm in 1935, the Ephraim Palais stood in the oldest part of Berlin. In the 18th Century it was one of Berlin's most distinguished mansions. Since 1762, it had belonged to Veit Ephraim, court jeweler and financier, who had been granted the royal privilege to mint coins. Since the demolition of the house in 1935, the fragments of the baroque sandstone facade have been stored in West Berlin, some 100 meters removed from the original site. Seen from the historical, architectural and functional perspectives, it was a controversial decision on the part of the Berlin Senate to reconstruct the Ephraim Palais in another location, namely in the southern Friedrichstadt, which had been very seriously destroyed through the war and post-war planning. (The former site no longer exists, eliminated by widening of the Mühlendamm). Here, placed diagonally to the Berlin Museum, the only remaining baroque building in this historic quarter, the rebuilt palace should form a new corner situation.

The spatial urban context of the newly selected site demands, as does the program of the Jewish Museum (a part of the Berlin Museum), completion of the reconstructed Palais in the form of a new extension. The conception signifies a contradiction of the new and the old. The present against the past through spatial experience, construction, and material. The present with the past through morphological affinity, modular discipline and physiognomical rationality.

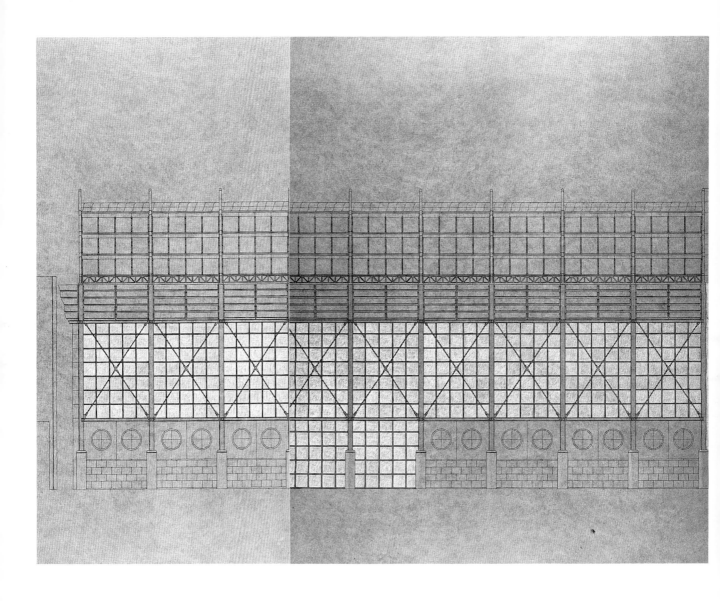

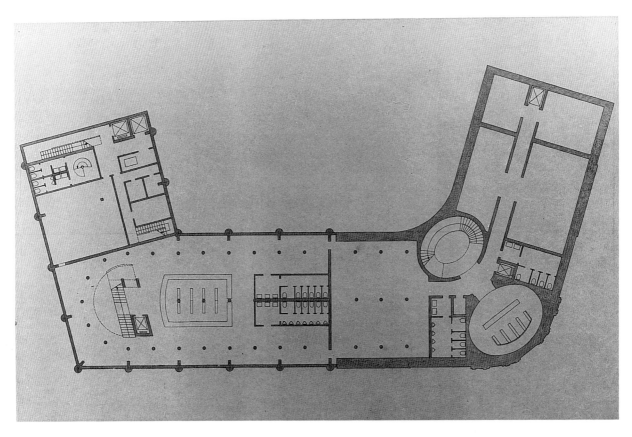

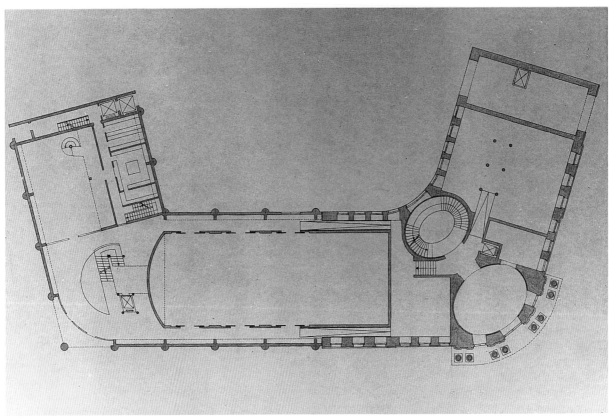

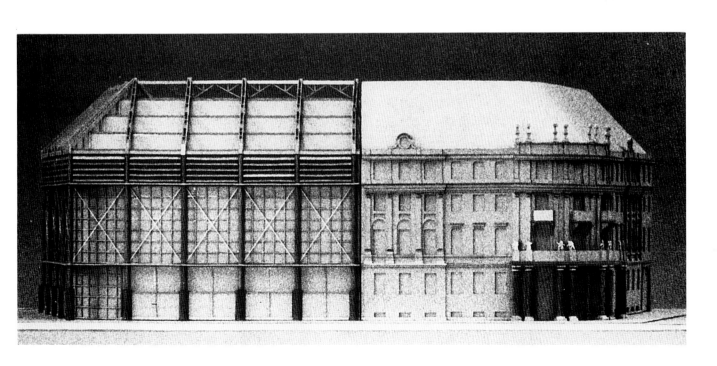

GERMAN BLADE MUSEUM AND CITY ARCHIVE

The threatening dilapidation of the former Gräfrather Monastery, and the fact that it hasn't been in use for years, were reasons for the City of Solingen to commission a study for a possible re-utilization of this site as the German Museum of Swords and Blades.

Utilizing the complete structural ensemble on top of the Gräfrather Klosterberg (Monastery Hill) J.P. Kleihues made diversified usage a subject matter of this study. However, it was not until seven years later that the first phase, alteration of the monastery, went into construction. It is scheduled to be completed by Fall, 1989. Any building for the Civic Archives still remains unknown.

VITALIC SYMBOLITY OF THE LEAF

URBAN HISTORY, LIFE'S HISTORY

THE WRITTEN LEAF OF PAPER, and

THE LEAF BLOWING IN THE WIND

The Gräfrather Monastery, together with its church and rectory, is an exquisite ensemble of historical architectural importance. Its special topographical situation, its urban and functional associations that developed over centuries in the little town of Gräfrath nestled into the landscape, have created a high scale urban-architectural composition of great rarity.

Quoting from reports of the State Preservation Authority: "The old heart of the village, situated in a narrow valley, is a harmonious scene thanks to slate, which covers the roofs and most of the facades. Framework can only be seen on sides of buildings opposite the weather. The catholic parish church, with its baroque structures built on a hill rising northeast of the market square, commands the Old Town."

The buildings of the present can only be dated back to the 17th Century, even though the town Gräfrath is older. It was called *Freedom* from 1135 to 1482. The excellent preservation of this village and the modest urban setting, having grown over the centuries with a very natural relationship for the landscape, deserves to be maintained and cultivated.

The parish church, the former monastery, and a number of houses surrounding the market square and in neighboring streets have been proclaimed a protection zone by the State Preservation Authority of Rhineland. Maintenance and the utilization of historical structures are however not guaranteed by proclamations; money is needed and long-term planning.

The upkeep of Gräfrather housing is maintained by individual owners, and the parish church is maintained by the still active church community. The former Gräfrather Monastery is civic property, having served a variety of purposes since under state ownership, and is dependent on and maintained by the City of Solingen.

The poor condition of the monastery and its use as the provisional Civic Archives led to a study in the late 70's which projected not only the preservation of the structural enclosure but created new functions, for four institutions; they are: the German Museum of Swords and Blades, the Gräfrather Church Treasury Vault, the Bergisch Art Gallery, and the Civic Archives of Solingen.

A quick review of the history and peculiarities of these institutions will help in understanding the urban plan and architectural design. Only one new structure was proposed for the Civic Archives.

THE GERMAN MUSEUM OF SWORDS AND BLADES

The basis of this museum collection dates back to 1904. The institution was used for study purposes by the old Vocational Institute of Materials as an archive of trade and artistic tradition. The German Museum of Swords and Blades celebrated its fiftieth anniversary when it was officially founded and named in 1954, and when it finally opened to the public in the former Town Hall. So it really was not until after World War II that a concept was developed to dedicate a museum to a vast accumulation of swords and blades, of all times and places, of cutlery from around the world, and last but not least, to dedicate a museum to the blades of the masters from Solingen. Since then the collection has improved and expanded, and is now one of the foremost collections of a specific subject matter in the world.

This museum requires a generous amount of space, which was available in the former monastery. The completely re-built interior will be finished by Fall, 1989.

THE GRÄFRATHER CHURCH TREASURY VAULT

The artistic value makes this church vault distinguished and its association, having grown over centuries with the region, documents its changing history so well. Of particular interest are medieval worship reliquaries, which were the impetus for Gräfrath becoming a place of pilgrimmage in the 14th and 15th Centuries.

The oldest object is a Byzantine Crown of Mary, which was perhaps the founding gift to this Monastery of St. Mary. A collection, comprised mainly of reliquaries and ostensaries accumulated up to 1500 A.D., occupies the main part of the vault, which also includes precious goblets, processional crosses, and holders for incense. One room of approximately six hundred square feet

could fulfill all of the exhibition requirements.

The premise of this design was to create a dignified exhibition space directly connected to the church but not integrated with the museum. An appropriate location was the upper floor of the northern church building. Thanks to the support of Professor Hallauer, the Chairman of the Gräfrather Parish Community, renovation of this space will be completed simultaneously with work on the monastery.

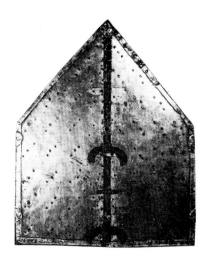

THE BERGISCH ART GALLERY

Up until 1933 the Solingen Art College was the center of artistic activities in the area. It was here, in 1931 that the Solingen Artists Union held an extensive exhibition of local work. The movement was revived in 1947 under the name "Bergische Galerie" (Bergisch Art Gallery). Since then annual exhibitions have been held showing the interests and activities of Solingen artists. Several hundred paintings, drawings, graphics, sculptures, and handcrafted objects comprise the collection of the gallery. By having its own space, the most important pieces of art could be exhibited. Changing exhibitions and a variety of events could also be organized.

The most appropriate place for the gallery would be in the former laborer's tenement, located next to the east wing of the monastery in the upper Gerbestrasse built at the turn of the century. The long, narrow structure is well suited for this renovation. The city decided, however, that for the time being the gallery could use two exhibition rooms in the former monastery (in the German Museum of Swords and Blades). From a financial viewpoint this is a very understandable decision, but extremely insufficient for an extended period of time.

In the same year that the Museum of Swords and Blades was officially established, the "Archives of the City of Solingen" took over the immense Department of Local History and Geography from the city library, and with it the whole library of the Bergisch History Club. The collection contains documents of the history of Solingen, plus the most important publications about the history of the region.

Council protocols, civic invoices, business licenses, protocols from the Tradesmen's Court, surveying scrolls, and state decrees, some dating back to the 17th Century, all belong to the civic archives, as well as an extensive map collection with valuable Solingen works and a large quantity of regional plans. The picture archive includes a vast photographic collection and the books in the library deal especially with the history of Solingen, of the Bergisches Land, and of the Rhineland. Finally, copies of every paper published in Solingen since 1829 are archived, plus an extensive collection of other papers. It is obvious that close proximity of the museum and archive should be taken into consideration.

On one hand, by being able to view the most essential items of the museum's collection, and being able to compare them with other selected objects from around the world, the history of steel in Solingen and the financial / social development of the area are kept in memory. On the other hand, direct reference must be available to the written history of the city, which is kept by the archive. This concept can only be possible by building a new structure for the archive, as an addition to the ensemble on the Gräfrather Klosterberg (Monastery Hill). The cultural and political reasoning presented here, and the design shown in drawings and models, are to be evaluated as a realization of concept and ideas.

The urban environmental design calls for two narrow towers, each square and of the same size, connected by the one low central building in which the library and cartographic collection would be kept. The stereometric proportions of the plan satisfy a general wish to enrich the architectural composition, to be provocative, but with great respect.

Language is varied and ambiguous: there are the dialectics of protection of an archive that is open to the public; the contradiction of a steel tower with a stone tower; vitalic symbolism of the leaf, life's history, urban history, the written leaf of paper, and the leaf blowing in the wind.

Next to the historic significance of the location is the ambiguous definition of its purpose directed toward the future.

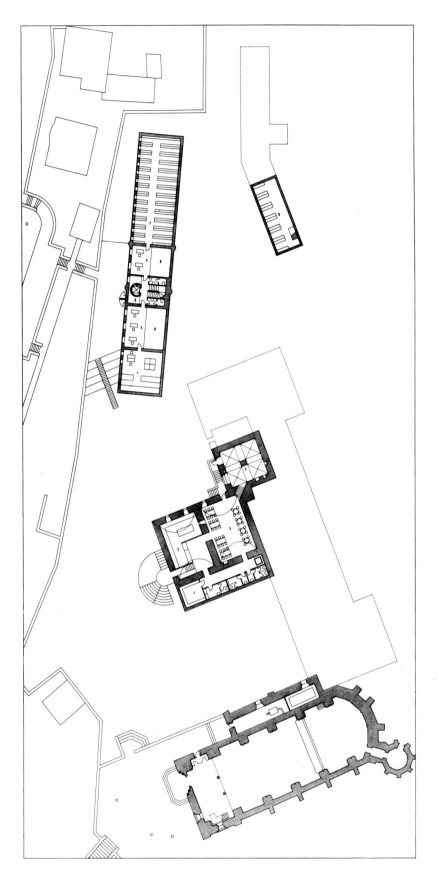

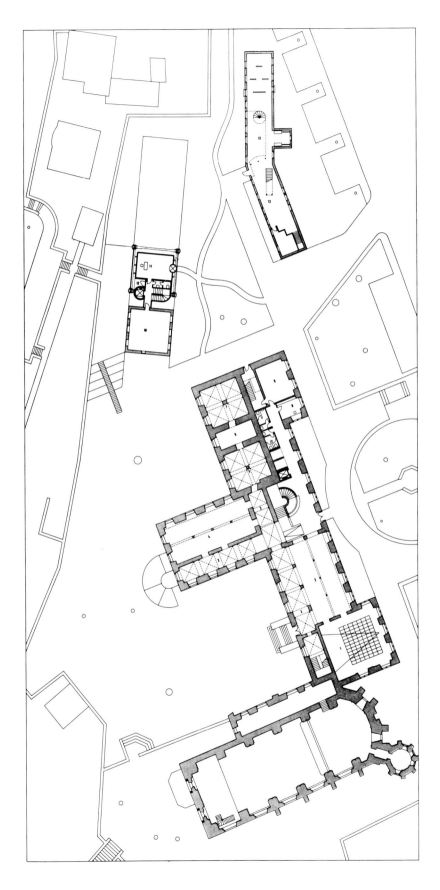

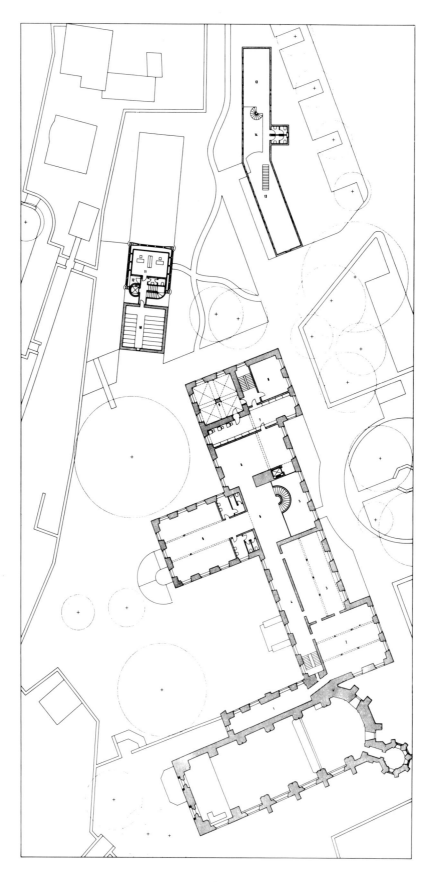

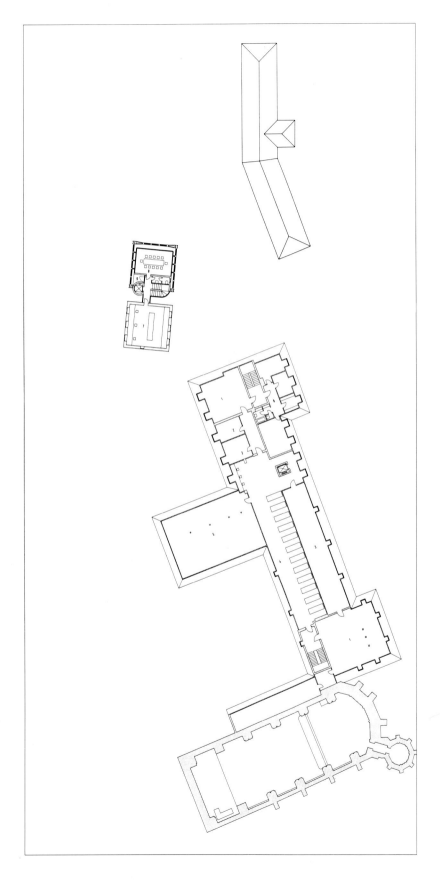

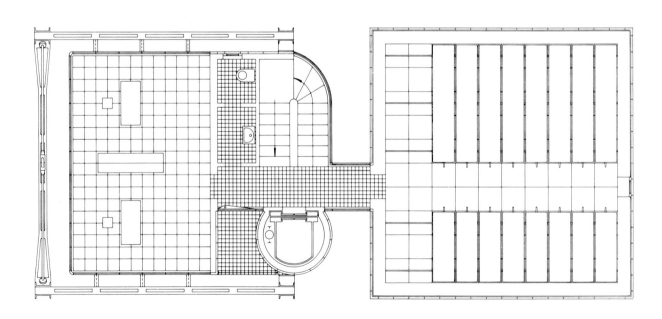

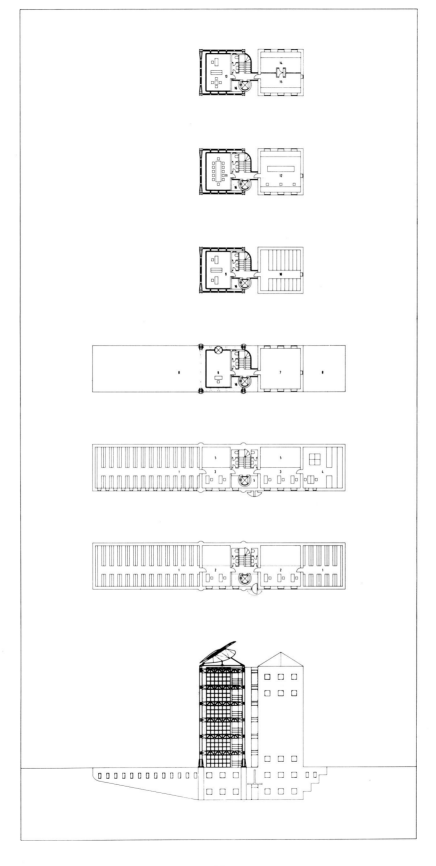

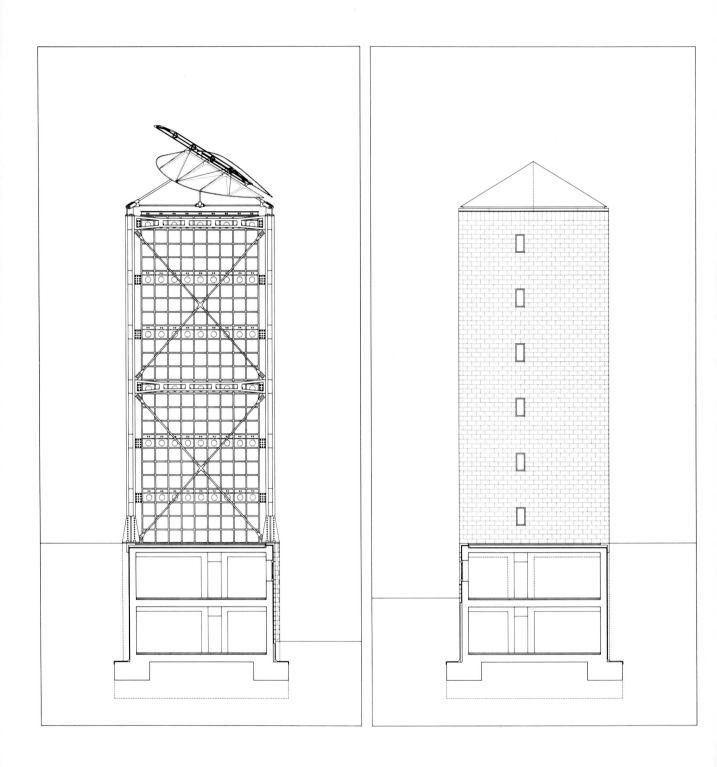

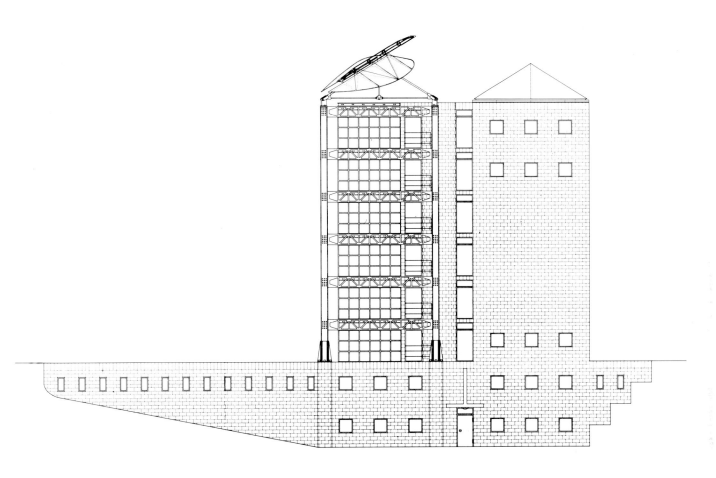

STÄDEL MUSEUM EXPANSION

In the Fall of 1985, J.P. Kleihues worked together with Frankfurter Aufbau AG (FAAG) on a feasibility study for the extension of the Städel Museum. The design was rejected, however, because it was contrary to the intention of the museum's administration to construct the planned extension in the form of a side wing.

GENEALOGY OF A COLLECTION

GENEALOGY OF THE STÄDEL

ADDITION, CORRELATION, INTEGRATION

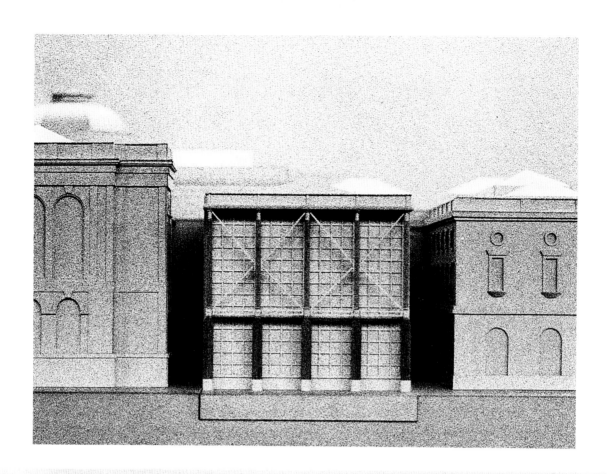

104

At the end of the 1960s, when the renowned Kraushaar Collection was obtained by Mr. Ströher and brought to Darmstadt, no one could have had any idea that this emblematic collection of Pop-Art pictures and objects, as well as other pieces in the Ströher Collection, would one day end up in Frankfurt. The existing need for an extension to the Städel Museum took on a further urgency through the acquistion of these pieces.

In conscious contradiction to the intention of the Städel administration to carry out the extension in the form of a side wing with a separate entrance,an alternative design was presented which allowed both the existing and new sections to be reached from the centrally located stairwell. The design wanted to realize a planning idea which would compress and emphasize the solitary nature of the historical construction:
— as the addition of body and space
— as a correlation to the spirit of architecture
— as the integration into the genealogy of the Städel.

The extension of the Städel which is now under construction has other aims.

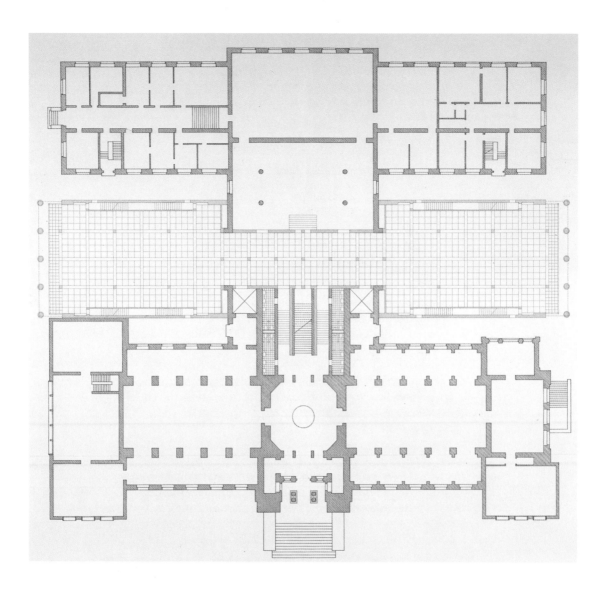

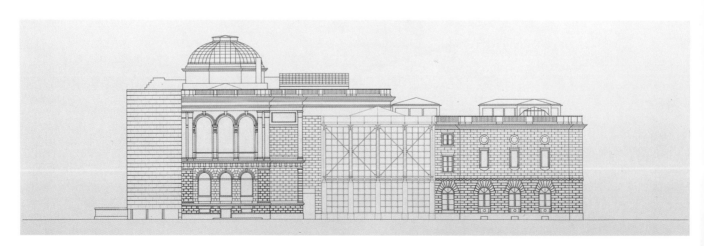

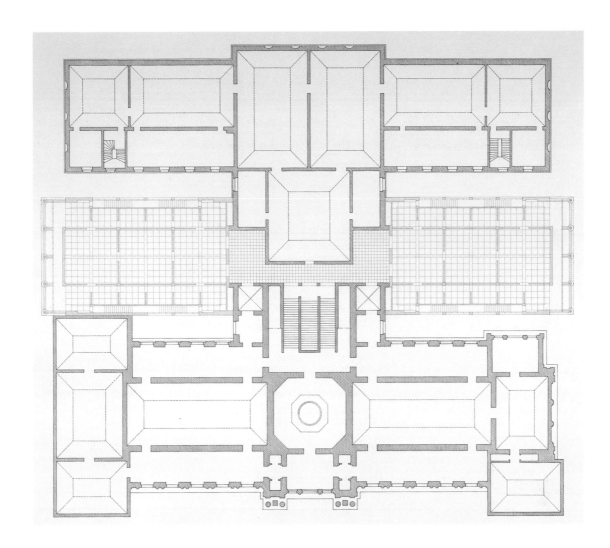

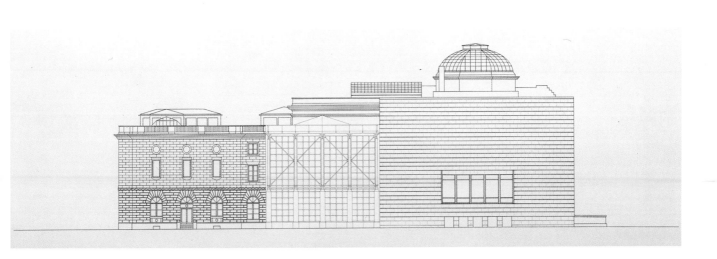

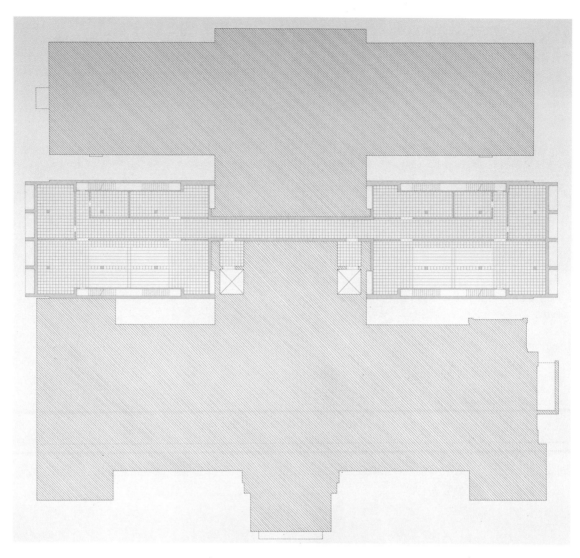

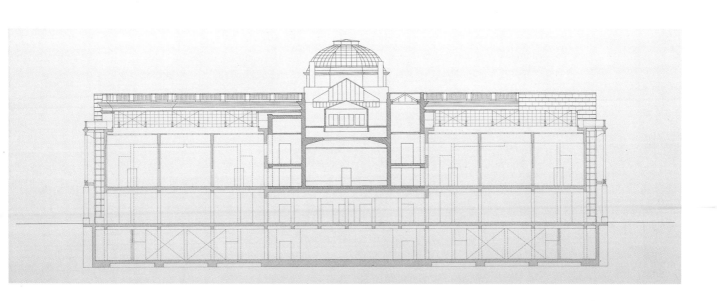

FEDERAL HALL FOR ART EXHIBITIONS

A competition for the Federal Hall for Art Exhibitions in Bonn, involving several phases of design, took place from 1984 to 1986. Three architects were selected to participate in the last stage of the competition. This work was awarded the Second Prize. Although the technical details were exactly defined and specified some of the jury remained convinced that the project could not be built.

MOBILE WALLS AND ROTATABLE ROOMS

PRESSED STEEL AND TIGHT CABLES

THE BUILDING; A TECHNICAL INSTRUMENT

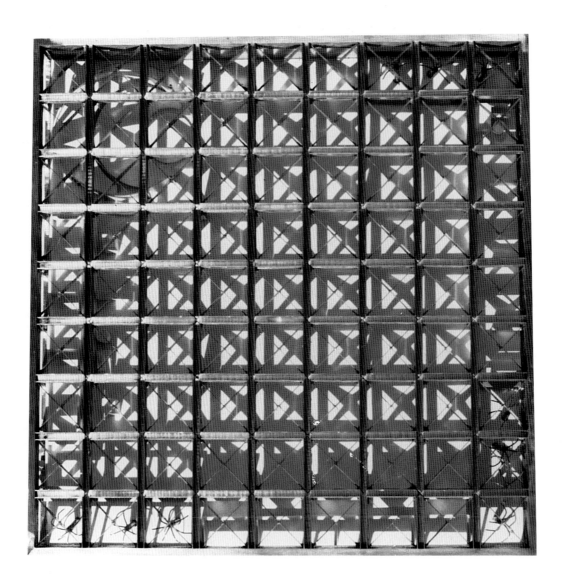

A gallery is not a museum. Programs for exhibitions are not predictable. The concept and exhibition of art and culture covers a broad field of different themes and purposes. Neutral presentations as well as artistic settings must be equally feasible.

The expanse of exhibitions changes just as well. Because of that, it must be possible for a mixture of installations of various sizes, just as easily as for one grand arrangement. These needs can only be satisfied by a modular structure, a machinery, which equally fulfills all the functional and representable requirements: a technical instrument, ingenious in size and construction, simply manageable, flexible and variable.

This conception is not defined by dimensions and proportions, or by specific materials or construction, but by utilization that fulfills a specific requirement, and achieves a desired setting within the structure. The system of modules and construction, legible in the drawings, is a commitment to this intention.

Twenty feet is the standard ceiling height, but variable ceiling heights are important for creating different settings. The ceiling system panels can be electronically moved by a synchronized, geared machinery. Two motors should be supplied for each panel, with their drive torque sent over electromagnetic gears to the individual pulleys. This enables absolute synchronized movement between two points, and, if desired, in opposite directions independent of weight. Service is no problem, as each ceiling panel can be lowered separately to the gallery floor.

Different space arrangements for different purposes are possible using a technical system of mobile walls. The system is composed of rigid panels, ten feet high and twenty feet wide that are hidden between the double beams of the ceiling system. These walls can be raised or lowered exactly, as can the ceiling. They are either part of the setting or just a display unit. The lower panels are divided into three parts so that openings can be made. A holding frame, flush with the floor, holds these in place. Smaller display panels can be placed in the conventional manner.

Bearing and non-bearing supports, in combination with the mobile walls, create the variable layout of rooms. The bearing supports define fixed points, the mobile supports can be pulled out of the floor with a cable, which is kept rolled in the crossing points of the roof beams. Should these supports not be pulled up, they then define spatial passageways. Skylights and side lights can be used differently to accentuate the space.

Climatization of the whole gallery is achieved by integrated ceiling and floor ducts. Every gallery space, approximately thirty square feet has an air unit that regulates the temperature and that supplies the floor ducts in the individual spaces. This allows for different climate control in each zone. Openings of the floor ducts are designed to not interfere with gallery installations. Openings can also be singly blocked or covered.

Three "quotations" of architectural elements supplement the modular system:

The entrance drive is a stretched *Court d'honneur* used by the gallery and the museum. Large transparent entrance gates offer a limited view into the space between both buildings, protecting the "Island of Culture" and drawing curiosity.

The "Garden of Sculpture" is a large, square space divided by surfaces of water, grass, stone tiling, and a variety of vegetation. This creates a landscaped system of paths and smaller spaces between the artwork, similar to the sculptural garden of Mies van der Rohe in the New National Gallery in Berlin. An interesting outlook to the surrounding area is possible from the terrace which circles the garden at a somewhat higher elevation.

The required "agora" needed for lectures, ballet, stage shows, pantomime, and cabaret is, with its elevating floor panels and changing settings, a *theatre absolute*. This concept, developed by Gropius for Piscator in 1926, could be realized by modern technology. The addition of several elevating floor panels would not be the only supplement; not only would the inner circle be able to rotate, but the whole theater itself would be rotatable, opening either to the gallery or to the Garden of Sculpture.

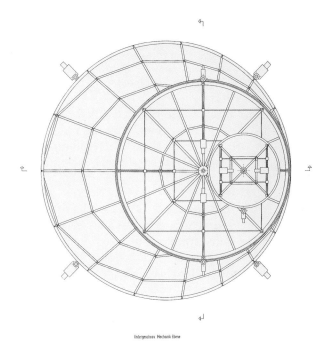

Untergeschoss Mechanik Ebene

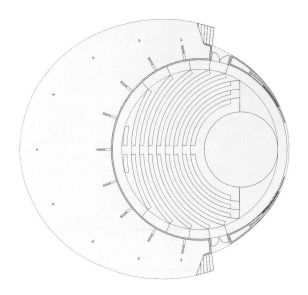

Erdgeschoss Parkett Ebene

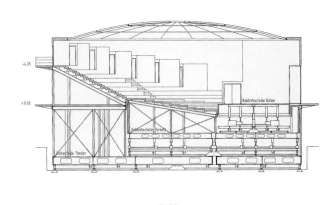

Längsschnitt

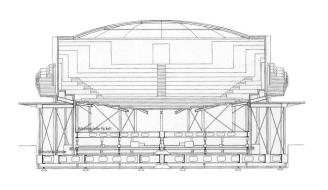

Querschnitt

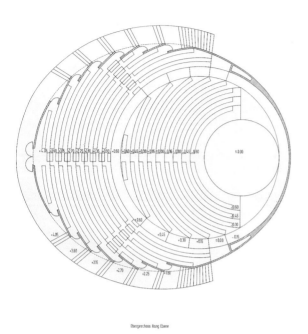

Obergeschoss Rang Ebene

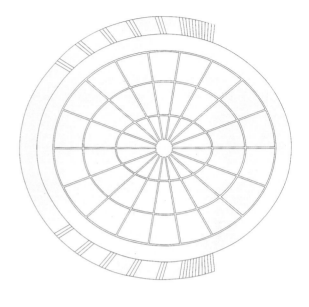

Dachaufsicht

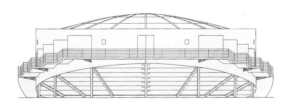

Seitenansicht

Rückenansicht

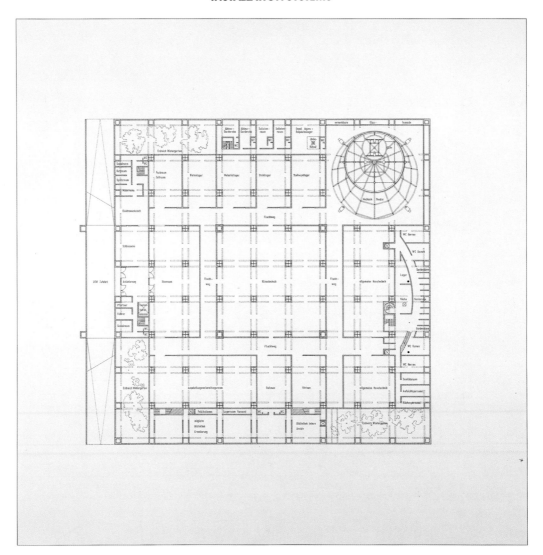

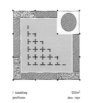

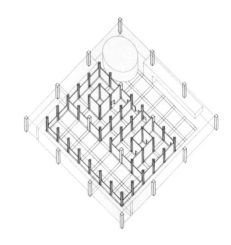

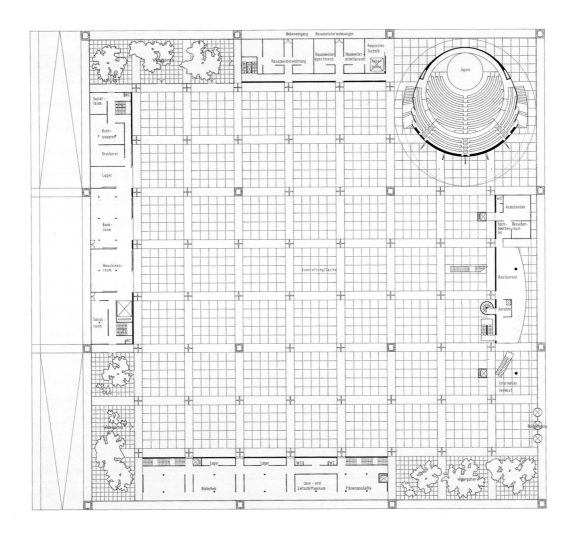

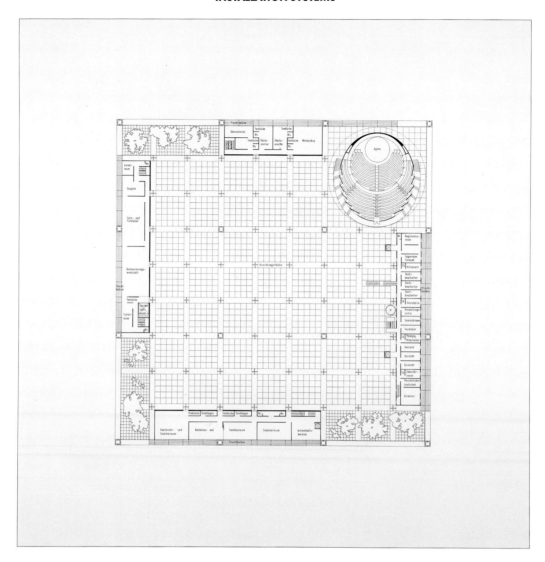

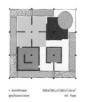

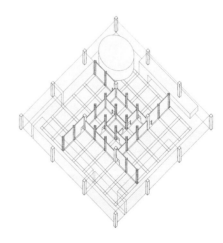

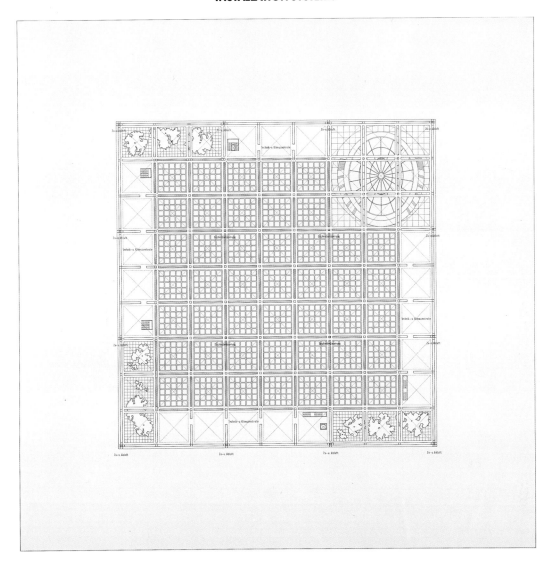

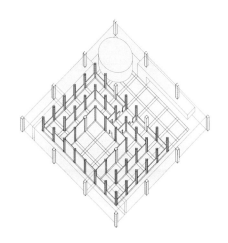

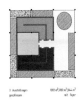

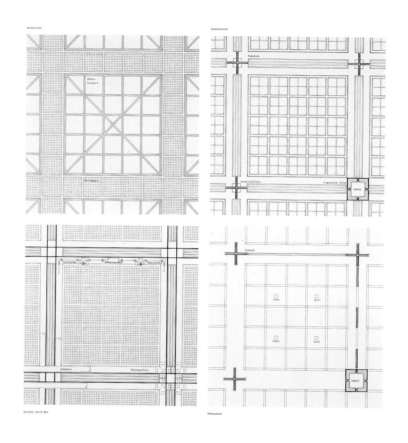

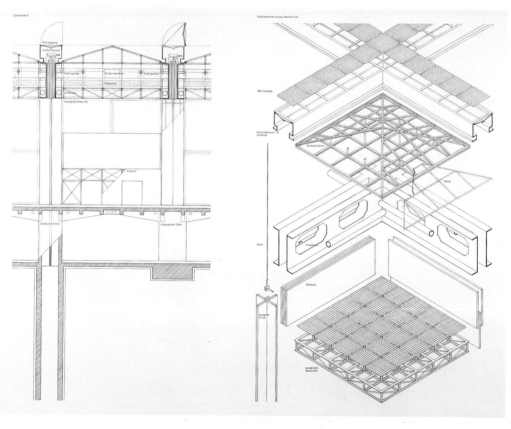

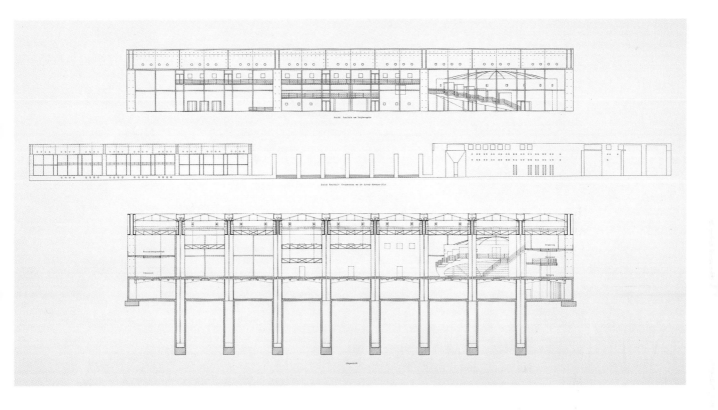

MUSEUM FOR PRE- AND EARLY HISTORY

In the Fall of 1979 an open competition for a new Pre-
historic Museum was announced by the City of Frankfurt
am Main. Several architects were invited to participate.
The following proposal was awarded First Prize and built
in the years 1986–1989.

CUT STEEL

NAILED STONE

MEMORIES RUSHING AHEAD

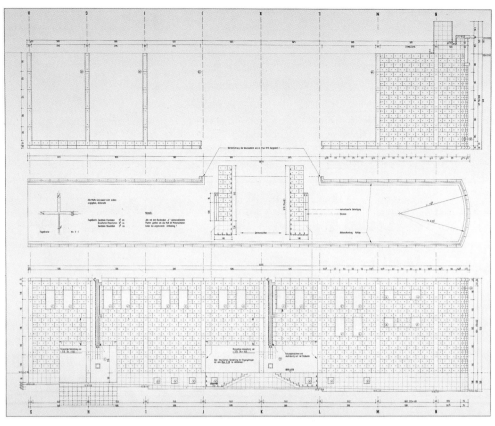

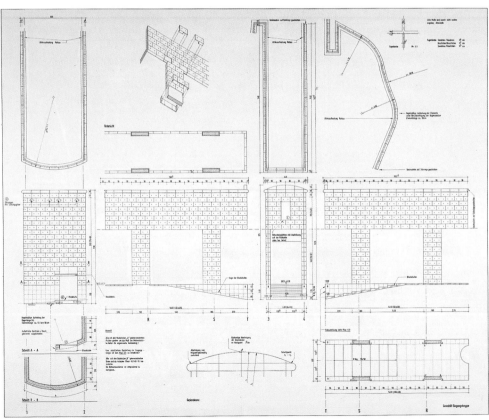

As more museums are constantly being built, new programs are being developed and expectations broadened. The demand can hardly be satisfied. The "socially" defined expectations of a museum are for the most part confusing. Discussions center on temples for the Fine Arts, educational spaces for the study of historical development and social conditions, "environment" museums, and on museums for interdisciplinary activities. But perhaps an archaeological museum can be just a simple place of perception and recollection, particularly since a greater awareness of history has been noticeable within the last few years.

The concept and practice of remembrance has supported planning, detailing and the choice of materials for this Pre-history Museum. Memories sometimes rush ahead, because the concept of remembering is originally dependent on the relationship between the rational and historical, with the prerequisite of the rational being independence.

This relationship of recollection, rationality, and independence, as indispensable and inseparable as it is, is uniquely defined by the practice of remembering: the ability to remember, the willingness to remember, and the intention to remember.

For example: Recollection of the Frankfurt Stock Exchange, built 140 years ago by F.A. Stüler; its distinguished Hall of Columns, and its striped facade of reddish-brown and greenish-yellow sandstone, all destroyed in the last war.

Recollection as a dialogical position, or to be more precise, the relationship of the traditional and the modern is diction and contradiction:
— parts of old foundations are reflected in the design of the floor tiles.
— combination of new dimensions with the floor plans of the historical church.
— structure in cut steel, in opposition to the restoration of the stone vaults.
— the tooth pattern of the stone brick reflected in the setting of the nails.

This museum is a quiet, provocative dialogue between the traditional and the modern, and a space for intellectual and sensual enjoyment.

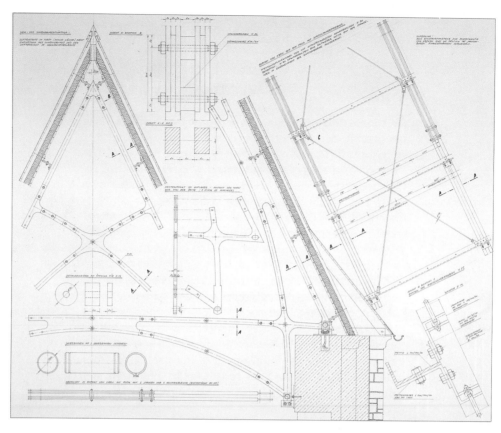

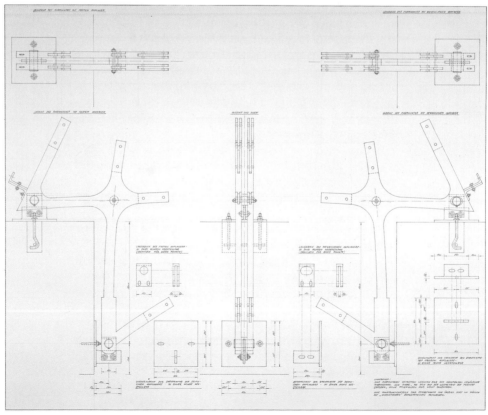

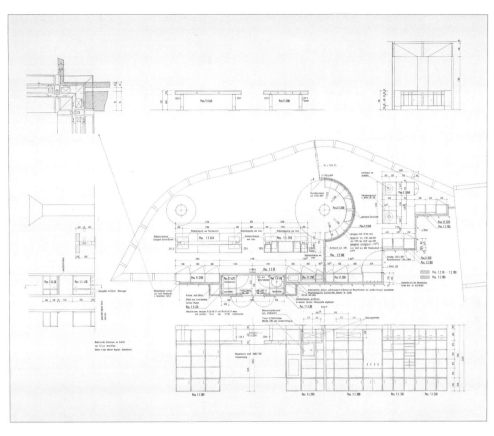

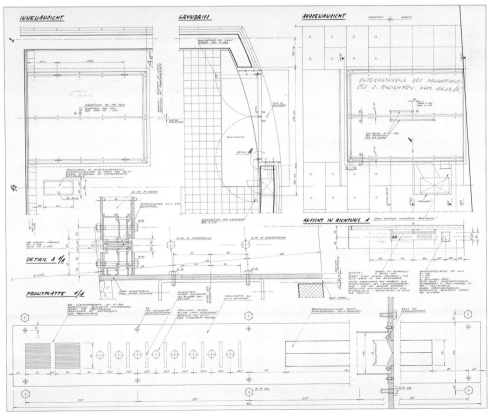

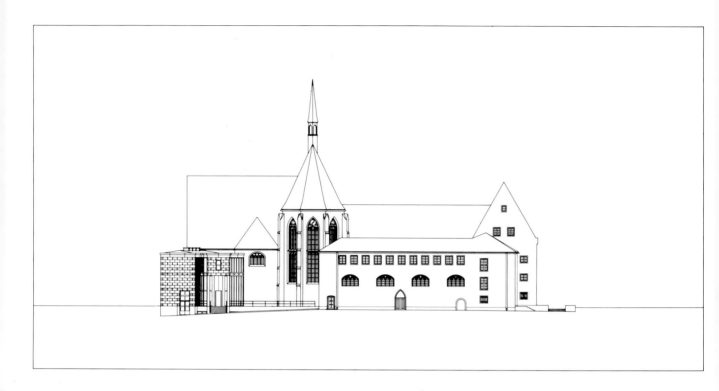

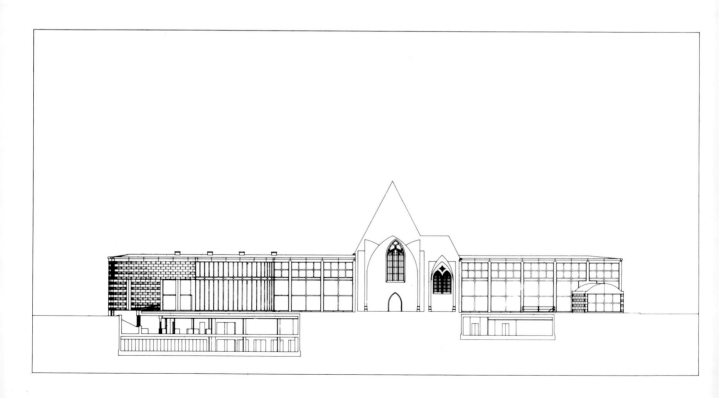

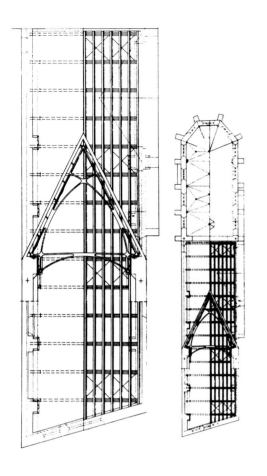

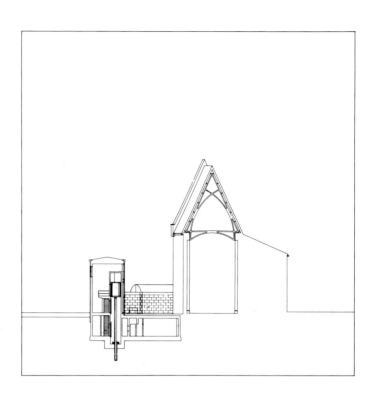

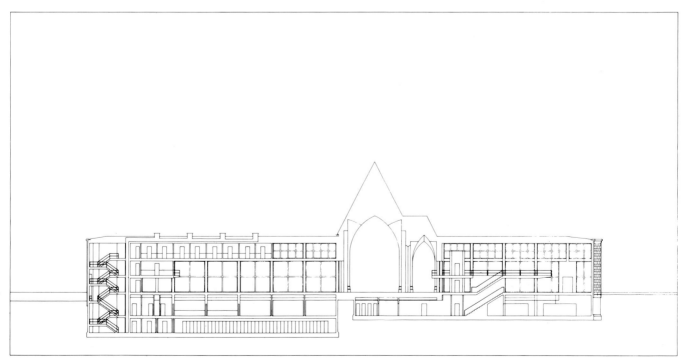

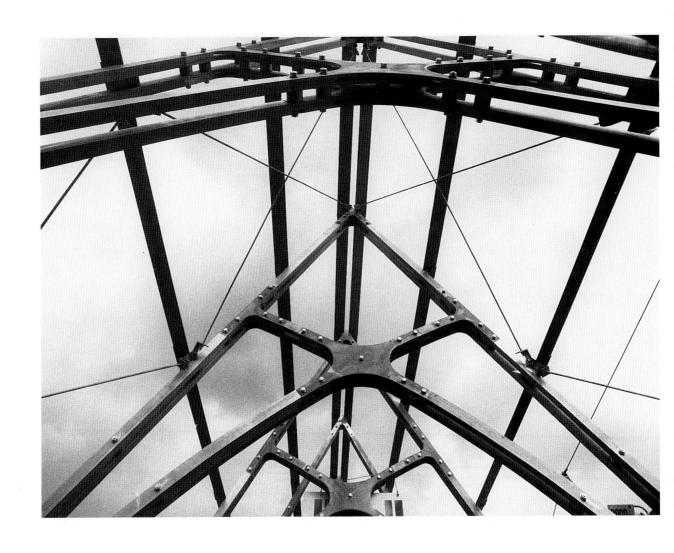

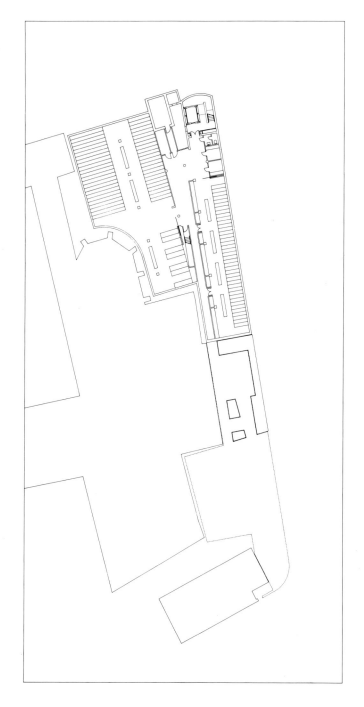

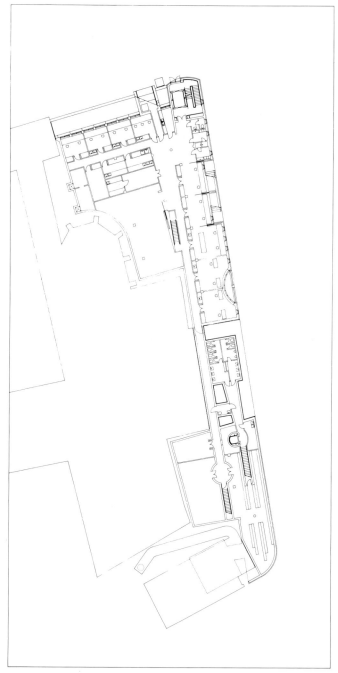

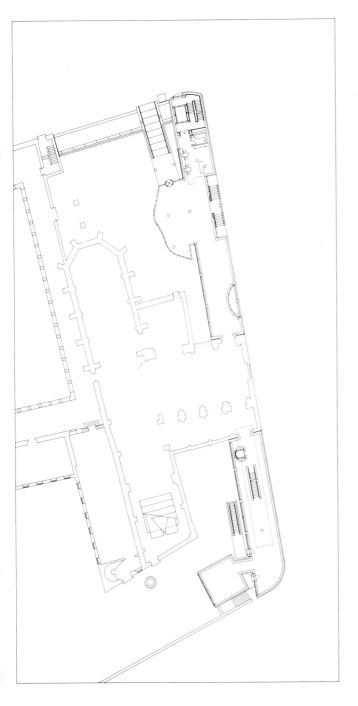

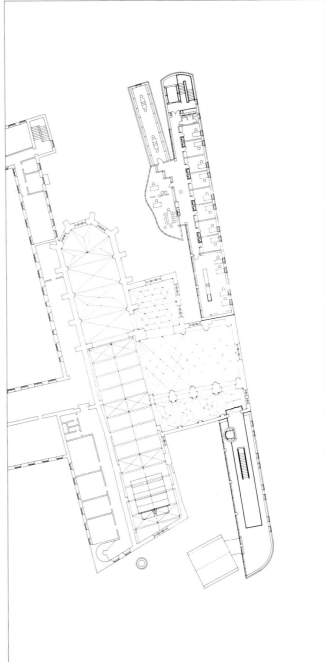

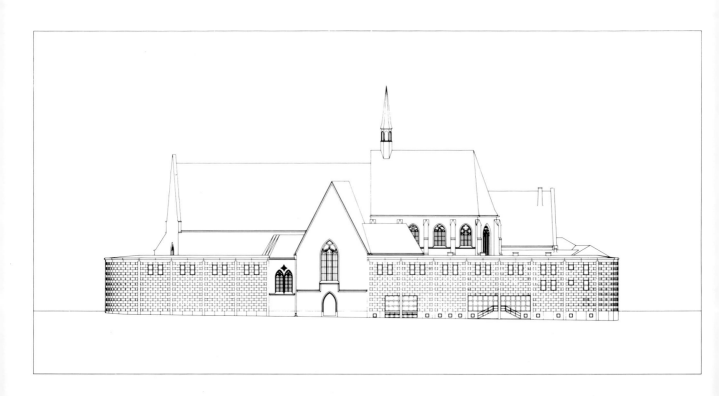

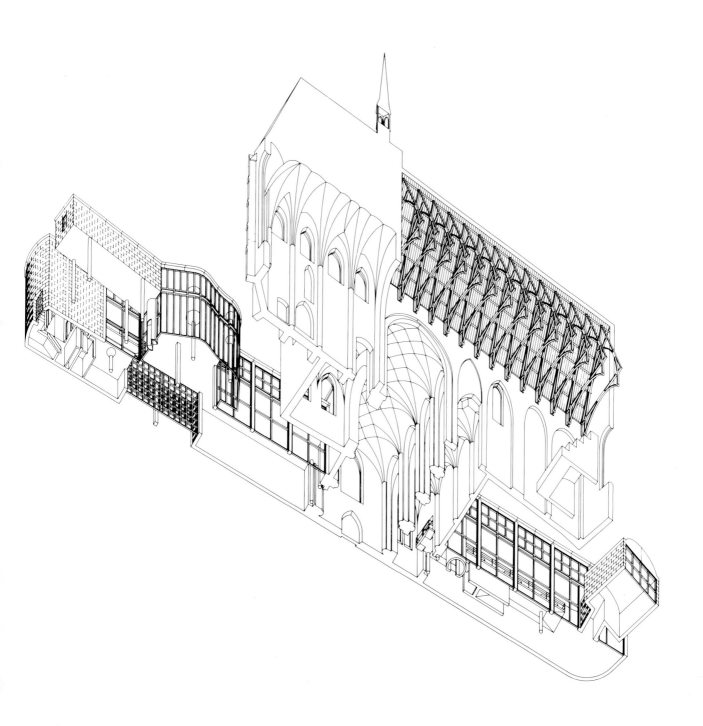

147

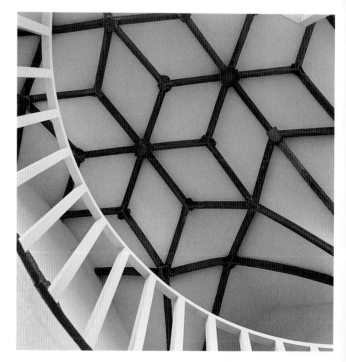

List of the museum designs (1972-1989) indicating year in which work was started, reason for project, its type and development and the most important assistants.

	Description and Location of Project	Reason for Project, Its Type and Development	Assistants
1972	**Sprengelmuseum Hannover**	open competition no prize	—
1975	**Landesgalerie Düsseldorf**	open competition with invitations, no prize	**U. Falke** **R. Hauser**
1976	**Aüsstellungspavillon für G. Baselitz, A. Kiefer, M. Lüpertz, R. Penck Documenta 1977 Kassel**	sponsored but not realized	—
1976	**Heimatmuseum Blankenheim**	commissioned to this point, only the first phase of construction (renovation and conversion of the former "Hotel Post") has been realized	**R. Hauser** **J. Flammang**
1979	**Ephraim Palais und Jüdisches Museum Berlin**	invited competition (4 participants) 2nd place; In 1989 there was another competition for a new Jewish Museum in Berlin, but at a different location	**M. Baum** **U. Falke** **R. Hauser**
1979	**Deutsches Klingenmuseum und Stadtarchiv Solingen-Gräfrath**	commissioned on the basis of a feasibility study conducted in 1979, conversion of the former Gräfrath Monastery into the German Blades Museum (including devotional objects) was begun in 1987 (first phase of construction) Opening: Autumn 1989	**T. Bartels** **M. Baum** N. Hensel G. Sunderhaus U. Kötter
1980	**Museum für Vor- und Frühgeschichte Frankfurt am Main**	open competition with invitations, first prize under construction since 1986 Opening: May 1989	**M. Baum** **T. Bartels** G. Sunderhaus S. Ni Eanaigh J. Kleine-Allekotte H. Rübsamen H. Schmittmann C. Wissmann

1984	**Bundeskunsthalle** **Bonn**	invited competition 2nd place	**T. Müller** **P. Attanasi** **A. Scholz-Weinland** J. Kleihues C. Kreplin E. Meinertz U. Schroder V. Suselbeek
1985	**Erweiterung des Städel** **Frankfurt am Main**	undertaken with the Frankfurter Aufbau AG (FAAG)	**M. Baum** C. Wissmann
1986	**Museum Lütze und** **Städtische Galerie** **Sindelfingen**	invited competition first prize under construction since 1987 Opening: Autumn 1989	**S. Gallant** **S. Häcker** R. Herrmann G. Sunderhaus
1987	**Museum Henninger und** **Städtische Galerie** **Kornwestheim**	invited competition first prize under construction since 1988	**I. Reimann** **D. Sommer** **R. Herrmann** H. Lenke G. Sunderhaus
1988	**Museum** **der drei geometrischen** **Räume** **Documenta 1988**	The Documenta invited a few architects to use a very small area to realize their idea of a museum. In the three geometrical rooms drawings by M. Lüpertz, G. Baselitz and "The Seven Columns of Architecture" were exhibited.	—
1988	**Museum** **der drei geometrischen** **Körper** **Groningen**	The sketches for the Museum of the Three Geometrical Shapes were drawn while I was advising the city of Groningen on its interconnecting canal and old town and as a preparation for planning the museum island.	—
1989	**Deichtorhallen** **Hamburg**	commissioned through financing by the Körber-Stiftung, the former halls for the flower market are being converted and will be used for exhibitions (primarily contemporary art)	**P. Kahlfeldt** R. Mcloughlin D. Schenkirz
1989	**Römermuseum** **Haltern**	invited competition no prize	**M. Baum** **M. Mensing** **O. Schmidt**
1989	**Salzburg Museum** **Salzburg**	invited competition	**J. Lenschow** M. Baum